CAIRO PAPERS IN SOCIAL SCIENCE
VOLUME 34   NUMBER 1

Egyptian Hip-Hop:
Expressions from the Underground

Ellen R. Weis

THE AMERICAN UNIVERSITY IN CAIRO PRESS
CAIRO   NEW YORK

Cover photo: Ellen R. Weis

This paperback edition first published in 2023 by
The American University in Cairo Press
113 Sharia Kasr el Aini, Cairo, Egypt
420 Lexington Avenue, Suite 1644, New York, NY 10170
www.aucpress.com

First published in an electronic edition in 2016

Copyright © 2016, 2023 by the American University in Cairo Press

All rights reserved. No part of this publication may be reproduced, stored in a retrieval system, or transmitted in any form or by any means, electronic, mechanical, photocopying, recording, or otherwise, without the prior written permission of the publisher.

ISBN 978 1 649 03231 7

Names: Weis, Ellen R., author.
 Title: Egyptian hip-hop : expressions from the underground / Ellen R. Weis.
Identifiers: LCCN 2022016017 | ISBN 9781649032317 (paperback) | ISBN
 9781617978517 (epub) | ISBN 9781617977145 (adobe pdf)
Subjects: LCSH: Rap (Music)--Egypt--History and criticism. | Rap
 (Music)--Social aspects--Egypt. | Hip-hop--Egypt.
Classification: LCC ML3531 .W45 2022 | DDC
 782.4216409623--dc23/eng/20220428

1 2 3 4 5   27 26 25 24 23

Designed by Adam el-Sehemy

Contents

Acknowledgments	v
Arabic Abstract	vii
Note on Song Translation	ix

1 Introduction — 1
   Hip-Hop and Rap — 2
   The Underground Scene — 3
   Research — 3
   Female Rappers: Outside the Scene — 7
   Conceptual Framework — 9
   The Emergence of Egyptian Hip-Hop — 11
   Reflections: Becoming Part of the Community,
      Part of the Research — 14
   Chapters — 16

2 Genealogies, Origins, and Narratives: Egyptian Rap — 17
   Narratives of Origin — 19
   Oppositional Cultural Products in Times of
      Political and Social Upheaval — 25
   Conclusion — 34

3 Degrees of Opposition: Hip-Hop and Expression — 35
   Habibi Music — 36
   "Rapping about Our Problems": Social Concerns — 38

	"The Powers That Be"	46
	"I'm Not a Monologist": Egyptian Rappers and the *Niqaba*	54
	"I'm Not Selling Shit for Anybody":	
	Oppositional Hip-Hop and the Market	57
	Conclusion	59
4	**Artistic Practices and Aesthetic Aims**	**61**
	Aesthetic Aims	64
	The Art of Hip-Hop	65
	Packaging	73
	How the Message Shapes the Delivery	78
	Conclusion	80
5	**Identity Formation in the Egyptian Underground Hip-Hop Scene**	**81**
	Identity and Symbolic Capital	82
	The Field of Egyptian Underground Hip-Hop	83
	The Embodiment of the Rapper	85
	The "I"	87
	The Hip-Hop Artist as an Agent of Change	94
	"You Are Not Appearing as Yourself":	
	Identity and the Market	99
	Conclusion	102
6	**Conclusion**	**105**
	Bibliography	**107**
	About the Author	**111**

Acknowledgments

First and foremost, I would like to thank my thesis adviser, Dr. Sherene Seikaly. It is difficult to find words that properly express my gratitude for her continued academic and personal support. Dr. Seikaly's enthusiasm for my research, encouragement, and critical attention to my work greatly contributed to this work. I would also like to thank Dr. Reem Saad and Dr. Mona Abaza for being a part of my thesis committee.

I must thank my dear friend, Laura Stahl, for taking me to my first Egyptian hip-hop concert. Beyond inspiring me to begin this research, Laura tolerated me throughout this process and patiently listened to my ideas as they came to me. I am indebted to her on a number of levels that I cannot adequately articulate here. I would like to thank Ustaz Ibrahim for his willingness to answer my questions at any moment, for his insight into the scene, and for the long sessions we spent discussing translations. Without him, this research would not have been possible. I would like to thank the hip-hop artists of the underground scene; I truly appreciate them for allowing me into their lives and providing me with the valuable information that I include in this study.

I must thank my family for providing me with the love and support that I constantly carried with me throughout my research as well as my other personal and academic endeavors. Finally, thank you Sam.

الهيب الهوب المصرى:
تعبيرات من تحت الأرض

يعد هذا البحث دراسة اثنوجرافية عن غناء الهيب هوب (أو الراب) فى مصر وممارساته منذ بداية انتشاره عام ٢٠٠٥ حتى ختام الدراسة عام ٢٠١٣ من خلال تحليل نقدى للعوامل التاريخية والسياسية والاقتصادية التى ساهمت فى ظهوره ورؤية مقدميه لدورهم الاجتماعى والثقافى فى مصر. فقد ارتبط هذا الشكل الموسيقى بنقد الأوضاع السياسية والاجتماعية واستخدام الكلمات والموسيقى كأداة للمعارضة والتعبير عن القضايا والمشكلات التى تشغل بال الناس. وفى هذا الاطار، يرى مطربو الهيب هوب أنفسهم كثوريين ونشطاء ومعارضين سياسيين وان كانوا فى نفسه يهتمون بالنواحى الجمالية فى فنهم من أجل جذب الجماهير وتوصيل رسالتهم اليهم. الأمر الذى يعكس رؤيتهم لأنفسهم وتعريفهم لهويتهم.

ومن أجل التعرف على هذه الظاهرة عن كثب، قامت الباحثة بالتعرف على ١٦ من مطربى الراب فى مصر الذين يشكلون جزءا مما يسمى مجتمع الراب ويمثلون تجارب وأشكال مختلفة من موسيقى الراب وعقدت معهم لقاءات مطولة تناولت مسيرة حياتهم وأهم الشخصيات والأحداث التى أثرت فى كل واحد منهم الى جانب رؤيتهم للتحديات التى تواجههم. كما اشتمل الحوار على كيفية اختيارهم للحن والنغمات وكيفية تسجيل وتوزيع موسيقاهم والعقبات التى تقابلهم وأماكن عروضهم وطبيعة الجمهور واهتماماتهم ونشاطاتهم السياسية وهمومهم الاجتماعية و تعريفهم للجيد والردئ فى مجالهم وآرائهم فى موسيقى الراب التى تقدم فى مصر والعالم العربى. إلى جانب قضايا أخرى عديدة. بالإضافة إلى هذه المقابلات، حضرت الباحثة العديد من حفلات هؤلاء الفنانين فى المراكز الثقافية والجامعات والحدائق العامة. كما صاحبتهم فى استديوهات التسجيل والمقابلات الاذاعية. ومن ناحية أخرى، تابعت الباحثة ساحة هذا الفن من خلال شبكات التواصل الاجتماعى واستمعت الى أكثر من ٣٠٠ أغنية راب من ٢٤ فنان وقامت بترجمة وتحليل بعض الأغانى أو مقتطفات منها من أجل التعرف بشكل أكثر عمقا على محتوى هذه الأغانى والرسائل التى يسعى مقدموها لايصالها للجمهور. وساعدها على ذلك اتقانها للغة العربية.

تنقسم الدراسة إلى أربعة فصول إلى جانب المقدمة والخاتمة اللتان تشكلان الفصلين الأول والسادس. يتناول الفصل الثانى أصول موسيقى الراب ودخولها إلى الساحة المصرية والعلاقة بين أشكال المعارضة الثقافية فى مصر فى القرن العشرين وموسيقى الراب الحالية. ويكشف الفصل الثالث عن أشكال المعارضة التى يعبر عنها مقدمو الراب من خلال كلمات أغانيهم ومحاولاتهم طرح بدائل ممكنة للأوضاع الراهنة. أما الفصل الرابع فيناقش تصور فنانى الراب للجوانب الجمالية فى أغنياتهم وما يمثله هذا من وجهة نظرهم. ويركز الفصل الخامس على علاقة مايقدمه هؤلاء الفنانون بتعريفهم لهويتهم.

Note on Song Translation

The majority of the songs I translated were in Egyptian Colloquial Arabic, although some incorporated words or phrases in English or Modern Standard Arabic. I generally transcribed the songs first and then translated them into English. I use only the English translations in this monograph. I tried to keep the essence of the songs to the greatest extent possible, which meant I took certain liberties with the translation of specific words in order to capture the meaning and I made some minor changes concerning arrangement. I also tried to capture the "flow" of the songs as much as possible; however, of course the translated lyrics will never read in the same way as the original lyrics. I was very fortunate to have the support of the artists themselves throughout this process; they were very helpful and patient and were always willing to provide further explanations of their lyrics and offer their input. When I refer to a particular song, I provide the title, artist, and date (either the date the artist wrote the song or the date it was released through social media). The second part of the bibliography consists of a complete list of the songs I reference in alphabetical order by the artist's name. If the song is available online (which they often are), I provide a link.

CHAPTER 1

Introduction

"The microphone is my friend; it appreciates my honesty." Deeb[1]

"I'm the microphone that raises your voice." Ibrahim Farouk of Asfalt[2]

"Hip-hop ain't dead, nah it never died, it just moved to the Middle East where the struggle's still alive." Arabian Knightz[3]

This is an ethnographic study of the Egyptian underground hip-hop scene and its artists' practices. The work starts in 2005, when many artists began experimenting with this type of music, and traces this music scene until 2013. It examines how Egyptian rappers locate their social and cultural roles, exploring the rappers' practices as both determined by power structures and a site of contestation. The study attends to hip-hop's location in the history of oppositional forms of cultural expression in Egypt and focuses on the artists' concerns with using their music as an expression of their opposition to various hegemonic structures. It also considers the importance of the aesthetic aims of the artists and points to various ways in which artists shape and position their identities within the underground hip-hop scene. Finally, it explores how artists approached and reformulated the genre in times

---
1 From Egyptian hip-hop artist Deeb's 2011 song "Masrah Deeb."
2 From Egyptian hip-hop artist Ibrahim Farouk of the rap duo Asfalt's 2012 song "I am Two Lines."
3 Arabian Knightz commonly open their concerts and music videos with this line; it is always stated in English.

of revolution and stasis to reveal how rap acts as a multi-layered form of expression.

By providing an ethnographic account of the Egyptian underground hip-hop scene, this work contributes to the broader literature on global hip-hop. Exploring this scene is crucial in that it documents how Egyptian rappers' practices respond to, engage in, or take part in producing the momentous historical events of these eight years. This research provides a critical analysis of the Egyptian underground hip-hop scene and the historical, economic, political, and social factors which contribute to the formation of this cultural product. It also contributes to broader studies on forms of cultural production as sites of struggle and political expression. To my knowledge, it is the only ethnographic study of this community of artists. While there are a few scholarly articles that mention Egyptian hip-hop artists as part of the broader movement of Arabic hip-hop, and one (that I know of) that specifically addresses Egyptian artists, none have taken an ethnographic approach to their analyses (Morgan and Bennett 2011; A. Williams 2010). I believe this approach provides an insightful and critical lens through which to attempt to understand the artists' practices. Additionally, the plethora of post–January 25[4] journalistic articles on the scene generally focus on the lyrics as a site to examine resistance and do not attend to broader practices of the rappers.

Hip-Hop and Rap

Throughout this work I tend to use the terms 'hip-hop' and 'rap,' as well as 'hip-hop artists' and 'rappers,' almost interchangeably. Typically hip-hop refers to a 'culture' and includes MCs, DJs, beat-boxers, break-dancers, and graffiti artists, while rap refers to a style of music. Hip-hop originated in the 1970s among African-American communities in the Bronx. In my research, I only focus on the rappers of the Egyptian underground hip-hop scene and I do not include accounts of the other artists who fall under the category of hip-hop. My interlocutors also note the distinction but generally label themselves as both 'rappers' and 'hip-hop artists.' I adopt this method of labeling because the artists view

---

[4] I will refer to the January 25 Revolution using the term "revolution" throughout this study, although I realize this term is debatable and does not properly capture the complex series of events that have taken place and continue to take place during this critical time.

themselves as engaging in a specific art form (rap) as well as taking part in a movement (hip-hop). They value the term 'hip-hop' because they associate it with a powerful form of expression which allows them to critically approach political, social, and moral issues. If I were to choose to refer to them only as 'rappers,' that would imply that I do not recognize the value or significance they place on their work.

In the Egyptian hip-hop scene, the DJs, beat-boxers, and breakdancers interact and collaborate with each other. However, integrating all these cultural workers into my research was beyond its scope. I found that the rappers were at the very core of this scene and their collaborative formation of the Egyptian hip-hop community serves as a crucial site of examination.

The Underground Scene

The term 'underground' is one that I adopt from my interlocutors. They assert that they belong to this scene, which they refer to using both the Arabic equivalent, *taht al-ard*, and the English term, which they pronounce "andirgrawnd." This is the broader music scene with which the artists identify. The underground scene consists of artists from a range of genres including, but not limited to, rock, heavy metal, and pop.

What does the term 'underground rappers' imply? The rappers I worked with assert that underground artists exercise the freedom to use language of all forms, such as 'street' language. A broad range of controversial topics, including political, economic, and social issues, constitute the music's primary themes. These artists position themselves as different from their mainstream counterparts. They assert they are telling "real-life stories" as opposed to the empty, idealized, and romantic stories that dominate Egyptian popular music. Defining oneself as an underground artist means not being attached to a record label; these artists represent and financially support themselves. This independence allows for greater freedom in determining content, promotion, and performance venues.

Research

Setting. I formally began documenting, interviewing, and routinely following the scene in April 2012 and concluded in June 2013. My interest in the scene preceded the start of my research, which allowed for greater ease and efficiency in its execution.

I feel it is important to make note of the political context in which I carried out this research, as it undoubtedly contributes to discussions, lyrical content, and particular emphases. I started my research in April 2012—not even 14 months after the "conclusion" of the January 25 Revolution when Hosni Mubarak stepped down after 30 years in power. During this time, talk of political and social change was common among average Egyptians and particularly prevalent in various local art scenes. Cultural workers still appeared to be highly motivated and inspired by the possibilities of change. Less than two months into my research, the first round of presidential elections following the January 25 events was held, resulting in the selection of two runoff candidates, former prime minister Ahmad Shafiq and Muslim Brother Muhammad Morsi. In June 2012, Egyptian voters selected Morsi as their president. My research continued for 11 months following Morsi's inauguration and concluded one month prior to the military coup that removed Morsi from power on July 3, 2013.

I conducted my research during a period in which opinions were strong, tensions were high, hope was prevalent, and change appeared attainable.

Period. I have chosen to focus on the Egyptian hip-hop scene from 2005 to 2013. I do not ignore the production of hip-hop before 2005 and refer to events prior to this year; however, the majority of the artists in the scene started during or after 2005, making 2005 a logical starting point. The reason several rappers began experimenting with this art form around the same time cannot be viewed as a coincidental "choice" independent of social and political factors. In order to provide insight as to why hip-hop started to surface in Egypt around this time, I give a brief overview of the major events that were happening in the region.

In 2005, Egypt's first multi-party presidential elections were held and Mubarak's opponent, Ayman Nour, won eight percent of the vote. More significantly, the parliamentary elections resulted in over a quarter of the seats being won by oppositional parties, with a majority of these seats going to Muslim Brotherhood candidates. Also in 2005, Palestinian president Mahmoud Abbas brokered a ceasefire with Israel, which is officially considered the end of the Second Intifada. Ariel Sharon, Israel's prime minister at the time, announced and implemented the removal of 7,000 Israeli settlers from Gaza. Nevertheless, settlements continued to expand, with an overall increase of roughly 40,000 settlers from 2004 to 2007. In the same period, the construction of the Separation Barrier, dividing Israel from the West Bank, was well under way. In Lebanon, former prime minister Rafic Hariri was assassinated, and public outcry against perceived Syrian/Hezbollah involvement in the assassination culminated in Lebanon's Cedar Revolution.

In chapter two, I provide a discussion of Egyptian hip-hop artists' assertion of the importance of their music as a form of opposition. While none of the artists I spoke with cited these events as push factors for using rap as a medium of expression, it could be useful to consider the relationship between the political context and the growth of this art form.

Methods. During the 14 months of my research, I spent a great deal of time trying to keep up with the constantly expanding underground hip-hop scene. Over the course of the research I formed relationships with many of the rappers in this scene. Each artist I met opened up doors to meeting other artists. This further evidences the importance of considering the artists as a community who actively and collaboratively molded the scene into what it is today. It is difficult to determine an exact number of artists who comprise this community; however, I would say the number of "active" members is around 25 to 30. Of course the number of rappers in Egypt exceeds 30; however, as my interlocutors informed me, "anyone can call himself a rapper and post a song on Facebook or YouTube."[5] Thus, my research focuses on this *community*, and 16 artists from this scene serve as my primary interlocutors. I consider my interlocutors as representative of the community—they consisted of various types of rappers[6] and I chose to include them based on a variety of reasons. I wanted to talk to veterans and newcomers, rappers who differed greatly in style, and members of the scene who clashed with each other. I felt that targeting these various members of the community would lead to more nuanced perspectives, thus resulting in better analytical material. Of course, accessibility and time were also factors in my choice of interlocutors.

I conducted extensive interviews in which I discussed with these rappers their lives, influences, lyrics, and musical tastes. Beyond the interviews, I was able to have multiple additional discussions with most

---

5   Interview with E-Money, March 2013.
6   I provide an in-depth discussion of the various "types" of rappers in chapter four.

of these artists. Generally, a "formal" interview would last between two and three hours. However, I met with several of the rappers multiple times after the formal interview. I had 33 interview questions. All questions were open narrative and usually led to additional questions and discussions. The general topics of the questions concerned the following: their methods for choosing music and creating beats, how they record and distribute their music, obstacles and challenges they face, performance venues and audience, music-related expenses/income from shows, their opinions about participating in advertisements, influences and motivation, what they consider 'good' and 'bad' in the scene, exposure to hip-hop, uses of hip-hop and other forms of artistic expression, political opposition/resistance, social concerns, revolutionary activities/participation, other genres of music in Egypt, and their opinions of other rappers in the Egyptian underground hip-hop scene as well as Arab rappers. I recorded interviews and wrote down points I thought were particularly useful or intriguing while we were talking. I allowed the rappers to determine the language in which we conducted the interviews. I held interviews at coffee shops, backstage at concerts, at recording studios, at my home, and at rappers' homes. I generally allowed the rappers to choose the venue of our initial meeting in order to create a comfortable atmosphere in which they could speak freely.

During my research I attended concerts, studio recording sessions, rehearsals, video shoots, and radio interviews. Concerts were held at a variety of venues such as cultural centers and institutes, parks, universities, and art spaces. While at venues, I was able to observe how the rappers interact with each other and comment on one another's work. I felt it was important to ensure the artists in the scene were comfortable with me, as I recognized this would lead to a more honest conversation about their lives and music. I had secured contacts in the hip-hop scene prior to conducting my research, which I viewed as a great advantage in establishing trust in the community. Sustaining relationships with the artists ensured the feasibility of my research and my access to the events, information, and materials in the hip-hop scene. Throughout my fieldwork, I attended social events with these rappers, and this provided me with insight into the extent to which hip-hop is an integral part of their lives. Of course, while these relationships were of crucial importance to this research, they were also a source of challenge. I worked closely with a group of people who have strong, not always positive opinions of each other. I found that some rappers questioned my intentions and "loyalty." As with almost any fieldwork, my difficulties lay in balancing a complex web of relationships, which required the consideration of other people's emotions and expectations.

In addition to fieldwork, I surveyed the Egyptian underground hip-hop scene through various forms of social media. I listened to over 300 Egyptian rap songs from 24 artists in the scene. Through close attention to the lyrical content of these songs, I believe I provide a representative portrayal of the commonly discussed themes. Song transcription and analysis was a key aspect of this research. I translated selections from around 60 songs (sometimes entire songs). The process of song transcription and translation allowed me to develop a deeper understanding of the content of the songs. The rappers often provided useful insight throughout this process, which helped to ensure that I understood their intended meaning. I visited the artists' Facebook pages on a regular basis to view new pictures, music videos, and comments, as well as to learn about upcoming events. Comments on Facebook pages and YouTube videos provided information about audience perception as well as how these artists interpret each other's practices. Photographs and music videos also allowed me to examine how the artists visually represent themselves. I also watched and listened to various television and radio interviews in which the artists participated.

My fluency in Egyptian Arabic was an asset in this research. Some of my interlocutors spoke English while others did not; I conducted the majority of interviews in Arabic. This allowed for comfortable discussion and exchange of thoughts on social and political issues.

Female Rappers: Outside the Scene

While there are female rappers in Egypt, they are greatly outnumbered by male rappers. They are not a part of the 'community' as I define it in that they rarely perform at concerts where other rappers are present and they do not interact to the same extent as the male members of the community. As much of what the rappers do seems to go against dominant social trends, I suppose engaging in this form of expression would have greater repercussions for women. However, this point deserves further exploration.

As I chose not to include female Egyptian rappers in my primary research, I would like to mention and elaborate here on their limited participation in the scene. The first attempt was a protégé-type relationship by the Alexandrian rap group Y-Crew, who founded and formed the female rap duo X-Crew in 2005, approximately six years after their own formation. However, their participation in the scene was short-lived—they have one song on Y-Crew's album *No Limits*, titled "The Girls Arrived." Their arrival and departure from the scene occurred within months. It is noteworthy that while they were technically the first female rappers to publicly produce music, their entire existence was dependent on a male rap group. The members of their male counterpart, Y-Crew, were completely responsible for their sound and their name, and they even appeared on X-Crew's one and only released track.

I can identify only one female rapper who was rapping for a significant duration during the period of my research. Missy Maira (Mayar) from Alexandria has been releasing tracks since approximately 2008 and continues to release a new song every year or so. The subject matter of her songs does not have much variation, and generally she chooses to rap about herself. While she has been around for a significant amount of time, she does not have any involvement with the community of rappers I discuss and seems to exist in an insular world in which she periodically writes a song and releases it via social media. Therefore, she has no place in this research.

Recently there have been several attempts by female rappers to become respected and recognized members of the scene. An up-and-coming female rapper, Soska girl, has released several songs in the past few years but has failed to become integrated in the scene. It seems female rappers come and go, which prevents their full involvement in the scene. As I approach this research as a study of a *community* of rappers, including female rappers as part of the study would be choosing to focus on the novelty of their existence. For these reasons, female rappers are not included in my research.

I feel it is important to mention female rappers here, as they will not be discussed in the remainder of this study. They deserve attention far beyond what I can give them, and the factors that prevent them from continuing to rap or fully integrate into the underground music scene should be researched and analyzed.

Conceptual Framework

This research incorporates the work of various cultural studies theorists, sociologists, and anthropologists. The critical tools of cultural studies, which attend to the relationship between culture and power, are concepts I have kept in mind throughout the course of my research. While I do not explicitly engage them all in my analysis, I will outline them here, as they were the starting point for much of the way I conceptualize the artists' practices. For example, Raymond Williams provides a nuanced definition of culture in which he considers how different fields tend to view culture. He asserts that in fields such as anthropology, 'culture' is thought of as *material* production, while in history and cultural studies, 'culture' is interpreted as *symbolic* production. Williams points to how these contrasting views of culture may confuse but also affirm the complex relationship between material and symbolic production; there is indeed overlap in these contrasting definitions (R. Williams 1976:91). Williams's definition of culture provides the tools to approach Egyptian hip-hop as a confluence of material and symbolic production.

Stuart Hall's approach to cultural production and identity as fluid processes that are constantly shifting and reformulating was also very formative. Hall asserts that "cultural production is in a state of ongoing flux, border crossing occurring and recurring all the time and constantly reinventing itself" (El Hamamsy and Soliman 2013:3). By approaching an analysis of cultural production in this way, we can gain a deeper understanding of the factors that push reinventions and reformulations of cultural products. Hall views identity as a strategic and positional process that is tied to historical and social conditions (1996:3). I consider these ideas in my exploration of identity formation of the artists.

Dick Hebdige's fascinating work on the subculture of punk artists in *Subculture: The Meaning of Style* allowed me to consider the extent to which the Egyptian underground hip-hop scene constitutes a subculture. Hebdige argues that "tensions between dominant and subordinate groups can be found reflected in the surfaces of subculture" (1979:2). He asserts that youth subcultures use symbolic forms of resistance, such as style, to challenge various norms. I kept his work in mind in thinking of how Egyptian hip-hop artists express their opposition to dominant ideology and hegemonic structures. Hebdige's work also led me to another conceptual tool, sociologist Sarah Thornton's "subcultural capital." I engage this concept in my exploration of the aesthetic practices of the artists in that it allows us to understand a hierarchy of values and taste that is not as bound to class as Pierre Bourdieu's "cultural capital." The concept of subcultural capital, a type of capital which one can gain from possessing knowledge of a particular scene, informs this research (Thorton 2006:100).

While I depart from Bourdieu's cultural capital to move slightly away from engaging class as the primary determining factor of taste, I turn to him for other useful theoretical tools. His work contributes to understanding the complex relationship between actors in the artistic world. Bourdieu sees culture as "a form of capital with specific laws of accumulation, exchange, and exercise" (Swartz 1997:8). His concept of a "field," in which actors struggle over the accumulation of valuable resources, serves as a framework for understanding the Egyptian hip-hop scene. For Bourdieu, a field "may be thought of as structured spaces that are organized around specific types of capital or combinations of capital" (Swartz 1997:117). In this work I argue that this scene functions as its own field in that it has its own set of rules and values, which can lead to the accumulation of various forms of capital (social, symbolic, and "subcultural"). Symbolic capital, power gained by holding honor or prestige within society, will be crucial in my consideration of the artists' practices within the field. Rappers place a high value on symbolic capital; they desire that others recognize them as legitimate artists. Bourdieu's take on social capital and the relationships that enable the acquisition of resources will help me to analyze the interactions of the artists in the underground community (Bourdieu 1986:252).

I engage these concepts and theories throughout the different chapters to provide an analysis of the artists and their practices. I draw on various bodies of literature to explore nuanced aspects of the Egyptian underground hip-hop scene.

Intersections: Global and Arabic hip-hop. In the following chapters, I have chosen to explore specific aspects of the underground Egyptian hip-hop scene. While my primary focus is on Egyptian rappers and their practices, it is crucial to note that Egyptian hip-hop does not exist independently of other global hip-hop movements. In their article discussing the imprint hip-hop has had on the world, Morgan and Bennett describe the emergence of global hip-hop "as a culture that encourages and integrates innovative practices of artistic expression, knowledge production, social identification, and political mobilization" (2011:177). While this applies to the Egyptian hip-hop scene, it is crucial that we consider how Egyptian rappers have created and nurtured their own form of the genre within the broader arena of global hip-hop. Fortunately, scholars of global hip-hop have thoroughly outlined the common features found in the production of hip-hop in various cultures, universal themes, and methods of interweaving the global aspects of hip-hop with local cultural values and tastes.[7] The existence of this literature allows me to move forward and address particular issues within the Egyptian hip-hop scene without addressing larger questions of global hip-hop. My interlocutors are indeed aware of global hip-hop movements, at least to a certain extent.

Keeping this in mind, research on Arabic hip-hop informs this research in addition to the concepts and theories I outline in the conceptual framework. I would argue that Egyptian rappers who started to participate in this art form around 2005, or after, were undoubtedly influenced or encouraged by some of their Arab neighbors. Most significantly, Palestinian rap groups such as DAM and Ramallah Underground had already been gaining popularity in the years leading up to 2005. Some of my interlocutors confirmed that they were fans of such groups but did not credit them as major influences. Regardless, I believe the members of DAM—who have been rapping about the oppressive circumstances in which they live since 1999 (Abbas 2005:34)—have served as models of Arabic hip-hop for many rappers in the region.

The Emergence of Egyptian Hip-Hop

A brief history. Although I mainly focus on the production of hip-hop in Egypt starting from 2005, there are artists who started making hip-hop music in Egypt as early as 1999. The first hip-hop group in Egypt was the Alexandrian crew MTM (Mikey, Takki, and Mahmud), who started in 1999. They secured a record deal and came out with their first hit in 2003, "My Mother Is Traveling" ("Ummi masafra"), which was an upbeat, humorous song about throwing a party while "their mother"[8] was out of town. Of the three members of MTM, Takki is the only one

---

7   See the works of H. Samy Alim (2009), Morgan and Bennett (2011), and Marina Terkourafi (2010).
8   They are not brothers.

still involved in the scene; he is presently plotting a come-back. Another Alexandrian group, Y-Crew, started around the same time[9] and was featured in Ahmad 'Abdalla's 2010 independent film *Microphone*, on the underground art scene in Alexandria.

Other groups formed around 2005, although their interest in rap started prior to this. The Cairo hip-hop group Asfalt started in 2005 with four members; it exists today as a duo and is one of the most popular groups in the scene. Arabian Knightz was formed in 2006, and other groups followed, such as Egy Rap School from Alexandria. Egyptian hip-hop is not limited to Cairo and Alexandria: artists such as MC Amin (from Mansura) and Ismailiya Soldiers (from Ismailiya) are also prominent. The rapper Deeb started with Asfalt, moved to a group called Weghet Nazar, and now performs solo. Zap Tharwat is another prominent solo artist who started rapping in 2008. I identify these artists as some of the "pioneers" of the Egyptian hip-hop scene.[10]

The artists I mention above and others of the Egyptian hip-hop community are part of a persistently changing cultural scene in Egypt. These hip-hop artists document and spread the news about serious issues and at times their music urges others to actively seek change. The stories they tell through their music offer their accounts of significant political events and social issues, which they claim serve as influence or inspiration for the production of their music. Some of the events that have clearly influenced hip-hop in recent years include the ongoing Israeli occupation of Palestine, the events leading up to the Egyptian revolution, and the pursuit of political and social reform in its aftermath.

Who they are: A note on class and educational background. While I have stated I do not engage class as a determining factor of taste in the Egyptian underground hip-hop scene, I do recognize that the rappers' backgrounds influence their exposure and access to different forms of music. Here I provide general biographical information as well as notes on social and educational backgrounds.

My interlocutors were between the ages of 18 and 31. Five of my 16 primary interlocutors were attending university during the time I

---

9   They say 1998, but others say 2000.
10 This is not a comprehensive list and the rappers greatly differ in their opinions on this subject.

conducted my research. Only two of the 16 had not attended any form of college and most were college graduates. Beyond my interlocutors, most of the rappers in the scene had some form of college education. Their educational fields varied, although I interviewed several who had gone to school for some type of engineering and quite a few in commerce or economics.

While the majority of the rappers in the scene were college-educated, most of them were not actually working in their fields. In this sense, we can view the underground hip-hop scene as a microcosm representative of Egyptian society. Several of the hip-hop artists were working in call centers, several were unemployed, a few had steady jobs working for companies, and others bounced from job to job occupying temporary positions to secure enough income for daily expenses. Only one rapper had a job related to the music field—he worked for a media production studio that often promotes and supports musicians in the underground scene. At the time of my research, none of the rappers were solely living off of their music, although it was a source of supplemental income for some.

These rappers generally come from lower-middle-class to upper-middle-class families. No one I interviewed was particularly poor or rich. After inquiring about other rappers in the scene beyond my interlocutors, I learned that most come from relatively "normal" urban, middle-class neighborhoods. Several actually grew up outside of Egypt—I interviewed three rappers who spent the majority of their childhoods in Dubai, one who was raised in Abu Dhabi, one who lived in Oman for several years as a teenager, and another who spent his entire childhood and early twenties in California. This information provides insight concerning the rappers' exposure and access to different musical forms.

I believe it is important to note that while the rappers participate in varied forms of employment and come from a range of areas, none of them represent lower classes of Egyptian society. None of them grew up in absolute poverty or had to resort to any form of manual labor as a means to live. It seems they all grew up with access to computers and television, and could exchange ideas and mix with the large demographic of people belonging to a range of middle-class neighborhoods.

Reflections: Becoming Part of the Community, Part of the Research

Throughout the course of my research, I transitioned from being an interloper to being a known "member" of the community, and my presence even incited a new way to measure legitimacy. As I already mentioned, I found this research to be challenging in that it required that I balance relationships and establish trust. However, this research was also challenging in that I, a female, was attempting to enter a male-dominated community and earn the respect of its members. Initially, I felt that people did not exactly understand what I was doing. I was often treated as a journalist during the first few minutes of interviews—receiving the typical prepared and prepackaged responses. I also got the feeling I was not the first foreign woman who had come around asking them questions. The majority of the rappers seemed to have a preconceived notion of how the interview would go, how I would act, and assumed I would have little knowledge of the scene. I almost always felt that, after they realized that I was doing something a bit different and that I actually had significant knowledge of their music, I was accepted and welcomed. Conversations were engaging and they seemed to enjoy exchanging information, offering their perspectives and ideas, and even attempted to help me "theorize" about the scene.

After working my way through the stages of acceptance, I encountered new types of challenges along the way. I found it difficult to "give back" to the community I was researching because Egyptian cultural customs of gender dynamics dictate that because I am a woman and they are men, they must perform specific duties. Naturally, because they were giving me the gift of their time, I felt it was the least I could do to pay for their coffees when they met me at coffee shops for interviews. This proved to be impossible and was always met with a "don't even think about it" type of response. I also wanted to support the artists by paying the entry fee to concerts, but was usually dragged away from the ticket counter and was told to "stop being silly." While I appreciated this kindness and generosity, I felt it was somewhat frustrating to have little agency within these contexts. I felt my gender certainly influenced the interactions between myself and my research community. However, for the most part, I do not believe that my gender had much of an influence on the information my interlocutors provided me with. A colleague of

Reflections: Becoming Part of the Community

mine once asked me if I thought the rappers were trying to impress me when they responded to my questions. My answer was "of course"—but I also believe that had I been a man asking the same questions they would have also tried to impress me because they are musicians who want to be liked and accepted. Therefore I do not believe my gender had much effect on the outcome of my research. I generally felt safe and respected throughout the research; I met many interesting people who were willing to share their stories and experiences.

One of the most fascinating moments of my research was when I realized that I had become some sort of marker of legitimacy for the rappers. After beginning my research and attending dozens of concerts, meeting with rappers after concerts, and being in and around the scene, people started to take notice. With each concert I attended it seemed that I accumulated new acquaintances. Most of the rappers, whether I had interviewed them or not, knew who I was and what I was doing. I generally kept to myself and stood in a corner with my notebook. About six months into the research, after interviewing several rappers, I started to be approached for interviews. I was simultaneously taking part in various types of field research, translating songs, and interviewing rappers, so sometimes there would be several weeks in which I did not interview someone new. On more than one occasion, I ran into rappers at the concerts of other hip-hop artists in the scene whom I had not yet interviewed. They asked me when I was going to interview them. At first I was surprised, but then I realized that they must know I am writing about the Egyptian hip-hop scene—and if I am not writing about them, what does this mean? That he is not a legitimate rapper? That he is not a significant figure in the scene? My initial method of securing interviews was to ask the last rapper I interviewed to introduce me to the next on my list, but after several months this was no longer necessary. Rappers came to me. In addition to being approached at concerts, one rapper called me, listed the names of several rappers I had already interviewed, asked me why I had not interviewed him, and proceeded to inform me he was ready for an interview any time. A discussion of symbolic capital appears in chapter five, but it is worth mentioning here that this experience certainly proved that "recognition" was a highly desired form of capital within the underground hip-hop scene.

Chapters

Apart from the introduction and the conclusion, this monograph consists of four chapters. Collectively they explore the artistic practices of Egyptian rappers through several lenses. Chapter two explores various narratives of the origins of rap and discusses continuities between oppositional Egyptian cultural work of the twentieth century and the Egyptian rap music of today. It argues that Egyptian rappers' work is influenced by their cultural memory, in which they draw from a repository of the work of earlier Egyptian cultural products.

Chapter three examines the multifaceted forms of opposition Egyptian rappers express through their lyrics. It focuses on the artists' dissatisfaction with various cultural, social, and political structures and highlights how their music and practices evidence a method of imagining alternative possibilities. This chapter will also point to instances in which oppositional aims actually reinforce dominant ideology. In an effort to deconstruct rap as some "pure" form of opposition, it touches on some of the artists' participation in commercial activities such as advertisement campaigns.

Chapter four focuses on the rappers' concerns with creating 'good art' and shows that rappers in the underground scene have different conceptions of what makes 'good rap.' It examines the artists' embodiment of their aesthetic preferences, their desire to create appealing products, and the relationship between their lyrical content and method of delivery.

The fifth chapter attends to the multiple ways in which rappers form, position, and create their identities. It explores identity as a fluid process and examines how rappers use external practices to help create an inner 'rapper self.' This chapter also focuses on the relationship between rappers' identity formation and the values of the field of Egyptian hip-hop, and points to ways in which we can view aspects of identity positioning as a struggle over symbolic capital.

CHAPTER 2

Genealogies, Origins, and Narratives: Egyptian Rap

On September 4, 2012 the concert started with one of the most recognizable voices in Egyptian popular culture, 'Abd al-Halim Hafiz, singing "Destined":

> *Destined, destined,*
> *You're destined to torture me,*
> *You're destined, my heart.*

Sharp beats and a voice rapping disrupted the soft and familiar melody:

> *A call to all liberals, Islamists, womanizers, and judges . . .*
> *Let me speak my mind but let's not speak about the past.*
> *The past disappeared with all its pain*

This song is "Destined"[1] by the Egyptian underground rapper Deeb, from his album *The Cold Peace*. Deeb blends old and new Egyptian cultural products to critique corruption and draw attention to the Egyptian government's neglect of serious social problems:

> *During the transitional period people bombarded us with sophisticated terms like "Technocratic Government" but failed to solve the real problems.*
> *Corruption was prevalent in the country and it stank like armpits,*

---

[1] Deeb translates the title of his song as "Promised" ("Mawa'ud"). However, after closely analyzing both 'Abd al-Halim Hafiz's and Deeb's lyrics, I have determined that "Destined" is the more appropriate translation.

And the cops were being commanded to execute orders like "Robocop."
I'm using the Arabic language to express myself and remind the people of the discrimination we faced.
Before the revolution if you spoke you would get whipped and thrown in jail.
The people who did this are now what we refer to as "remnants of the regime."
The current government is complacent and ignoring the real issues.

We export our gas, Gaza is still under siege, sexual harassment is still an everyday occurrence, just ask our sisters!
It turns out we're the majority and you're the minority.
Before banning porn sites, tell us who the "third party" is!
They asked me "What is humanity?" and I told them it is a human and his intentions.

Destined to have a better life because the one we're living today isn't rosy...
Stand by me or else we'll die,
Shout out loud: "No to the rule of monkeys, this is the time for lions!"

Deeb later compares himself to another Egyptian musician, Sayyid Mekkawi, who rose to fame in the 1950s and was also known for addressing the concerns of the people:

I'm not an amateur; I'm a musician like Sayyid Mekkawi.
Sayyid told us a lot of things but you weren't listening.

Attending underground Egyptian hip-hop concerts provides aural and visual experiences that reveal the ambiguities, complexities, and constantly shifting character of seemingly self-evident categories and labels. Egyptian hip-hop is a collaborative product of cultural workers who have combined specific elements to create a completely new and nuanced style of hip-hop. Deeb's juxtaposition of the 'Abd al-Halim Hafiz song and the contrasting beats, the references to other musicians who used their music as opposition, and the discussion of Egyptian political concerns all point to Egyptian hip-hop's unique qualities.

This chapter explores Egyptian hip-hop's location in the broader history of cultural expression and opposition in Egypt. By examining the continuities between this new form of expression and other oppositional Egyptian cultural products of the twentieth century, I question the scholarly narratives on global hip-hop as well as the narratives of the Egyptian hip-hop artists themselves. These narratives, in which people try to make sense of how Egyptian hip-hop came to be, overlook important influences that contribute to the formation of the artists' work. Egyptian rappers are not simply appropriating Western hip-hop,[2] nor are they consciously carrying on Egyptian or Arab "traditions." Rather, they are drawing on a variety of influences including archives of cultural memory.[3] Indeed, "memory plays an important role in various areas of social practice" (Erll 2011:1), including in the production of new cultural products. The work of important cultural figures as well as techniques and styles of earlier cultural work permeate the Egyptian underground hip-hop scene. Furthermore, cultural products take on a life of their own; people continue to reference them in relation to their daily experiences, rework them in the formation of new cultural products, and recycle them to express their feelings at specific moments.

Narratives of Origin

This chapter will present a genealogy of Egyptian hip-hop. It questions the common assumptions on the emergence of this form of cultural expression. Egyptian rappers use their music as a platform to speak about their opinions, frustrations, and concerns with the political and social circumstances in their country. Of course it is also important to note that the themes of Egyptian underground hip-hop are not limited to social and political issues. Moreover, the market and commodification also play an important role in shaping the content of the artists' music. Additionally, artists are not only concerned with the messages

---

2 I could possibly replace "Western" with "American" (the consensus is that hip-hop originated in the US), but the rappers themselves generally refer to hip-hop as *gharbi* (Western), so I choose to adopt this broader term.

3 There are various definitions of 'cultural memory' within the fields of memory and media studies. Here, I use this term to refer to an archive of cultural work that one accumulates from direct or indirect exposure to the work of praised cultural icons. For example, people throughout Egypt and the Arab world are familiar with Arab figures such as 'Abd al-Halim Hafiz, Umm Kulthum, and Fayruz, among others.

they send through their lyrics, but also with the aesthetic value of the music they produce. However, most of the scholarship on global hip-hop identifies the overarching themes as social and political critique, commonly associating the genre with opposition.[4] Some scholars point to the similarities between Arab and Western hip-hop as clear evidence of Arab rappers using and appropriating the Western 'model' of hip-hop to discuss issues in their own societies.[5] Egyptian hip-hop and other forms of global hip-hop most certainly share common features. However, focusing on these similarities leads to an overdetermined emphasis on mimesis, which confines the exploration of hip-hop as a mode of Egyptian cultural work. There has been a tendency to perceive global hip-hop as imitations of Western hip-hop rather than analyzing the local factors that contribute to the emergence of the local form. Therefore, this research will contribute to this literature on hip-hop by exploring it not as a shallow surface that reflects the West, but rather as a set of practices and ideas that can reveal both historical and cultural commonalities, differences, and specificities.

This chapter will examine the oppositional music and poetry that cultural workers produced during the 1919 Revolution and during the 1950s, 1960s, and 1970s. Are there continuities between Egyptian hip-hop's responses to and productions of momentous historical moments and earlier cultural work? From a historical perspective, this research contributes to the broader literature on the culture of protest in Egypt. There are valuable scholarly contributions on Egyptian cultural work as a site of opposition and resistance through the exploration of colloquial poetry, theater, novels, music, and protest chants. However, as Egyptian hip-hop is a relatively new form of cultural expression, there

---

4   I do not disagree that many hip-hop artists around the world use their music as opposition, and I also discuss Egyptian rappers using this art form to express various degrees of opposition (see chapter three). I am simply pointing out that the majority of scholarship on the international hip-hop scene focuses on the genre as a site of opposition (as I do in parts of this study). However, I also feel it is crucial to not romanticize the genre as pure "resistance" and to explore the artists' concerns with aesthetics as well as the relationship between opposition and the market.

5   See Kahf (2007), Bennet (1999), and A. Williams (2010). These articles provide valuable insight and even discuss the formation of the music at a local level. I mention this only because I feel it is important to shift the focus from hip-hop as a Western product that rappers around the globe "localize" or "appropriate" in order to examine possible continuities between hip-hop and local cultural products.

Narratives of Origin

are currently no studies that attempt to trace this genre. The only scholarly article on the Egyptian hip-hop scene, "We Ain't Terrorists but We Droppin' Bombs: Language Use and Localization in Egyptian Hip Hop" by Angela Williams, provides some useful insight: "The spread of rap music and hip-hop culture cannot only be understood as an American cultural import. Nor is it solely the manifestation of an indigenous art form and local expressive traditions" (A. Williams 2010:68). However, Williams focuses on the "localization" of Egyptian hip-hop, which inherently assumes Egyptian rappers took an "original" form and used local cultural and linguistic elements to make it their own. This work will challenge that narrative.

While I am interested in locating Egyptian hip-hop in other forms of oppositional cultural production from the twentieth century in Egypt, I will not claim that these are the "origins" of this new cultural product. Ahmad Mikki, the only mainstream rapper[6] in Egypt (as of now), attempts to trace the origins of rap to the Arab world in the intro song to his album *Originally Arab*. The introduction starts with the sound of horses neighing and a man shouting out a poem in classical Arabic. Mikki attempts to draw a lineage from the classical Arabic poetry of the Arabian Peninsula to the rap music of today. His narrative,[7] which he tells over dramatic music, is that Arabs were the first people in the world to have lyrical battles with poetry in the markets. After continuing to develop the art of poetry, Arabs founded prosody (*'ilm al-'arud*), in which they started to create systems of rhyming, rhythm, and intonation. Mikki attributes this field to al-Khalil ibn Ahmad al-Farahidi, an Arab lexicographer and philologist from the eighth century. He claims that al-Farahidi was inspired to create systems of rhythm by the sounds he heard in the blacksmith markets. By way of trade, Africans discovered and adopted this art form, as rhythm was already a "natural" part

---

[6] Ahmad Mikki is both an actor in Egyptian mainstream cinema and a rapper; he was already a well-known actor when he secured a record deal for his first rap album. He is the only Egyptian rapper (in Egypt) who currently has a record deal, although other rappers or rap groups have previously been connected to record labels. MTM, the first hip-hop group in Egypt, actually secured a record deal in 2003. I focus primarily on the underground hip-hop community in Egypt; however, I feel Mikki's narrative is relevant to this research.

[7] I provide a summary of the detailed narrative from the two-and-a-half minute intro song.

of their culture. When Christopher Columbus discovered America and brought slaves with him from Africa, this art form arrived in America.[8] The slaves used it to talk about their problems. When it moved into mainstream culture, Americans called it rap. Americans claim this form of expression belongs to them, but the truth, according to Mikki, is that it is originally Arab.

Mikki attempts to link the genre to "Arab practices." His narrative of Arab origins is a claim to authenticity. It is the direct opposite of the more prevailing claim of Western origins, and is equally problematic. Egyptian underground hip-hop is imbued with nuanced influences from inside and outside of the Arab world. Walter Armbrust's work on Egyptian popular culture shows how artists, practitioners, and consumers produce and consume popular culture in Egypt. Armbrust's work explores the formation of Egyptian popular culture as a complicated balance of historical and cultural elements specific to Egypt, influence from the West, and contestation of this influence (1996:3). In examining the formation and emergence of Egyptian hip-hop, I consider these factors, including some significant oppositional cultural products from the twentieth century.

"**I have a theory.**" When I sat with Takki, an Egyptian rapper who was part of the first Egyptian hip-hop group, which he created in 1999, I learned that he was very enthusiastic about my research and the idea of examining hip-hop from an academic perspective. He has become accustomed to interviews since his first album came out in 2003, and the media have been giving the Egyptian underground hip-hop scene a fair amount of attention during 2011–2012. This time was different. He told me that our conversation felt like a therapy session. He was finally able to discuss the past thirteen years of his life as a rapper in addition to his ideas about "the way things worked." He asked me to explain myself; he wanted to know more about my project and why I was so interested in his opinions. As I was explaining, I mentioned the word 'theory.' He interrupted me:

---

8   Columbus did not take African slaves to America. He set up production systems on Caribbean islands that used the local populations as slaves. Slaves did not start coming to the New World from Africa until 1619. But this is a part of Mikki's narrative and we must keep it as is despite historical inaccuracies, because it draws attention to how these rappers perceive the origins of hip-hop.

Narratives of Origin

> *Theory? I have a theory. History repeats itself. Hip-hop started in the eighties in America and it started here in 2000, so that's like a twenty-year difference between us and the origins of hip-hop. So what happened was our music reflected the same values and ideas [that American hip-hop reflected in the eighties]. So the beats were old-school, the flow was old-school; that was the only way it could come out here in Egypt because we can't just start with the same level they were at in America [in 2000]. We had to do it one step at a time so that people wouldn't be overwhelmed by this type of music. It wouldn't have worked if the first rapper they heard was rapping really fast . . . for example, if someone like E-Money[9] was the first one to come out, it wouldn't have worked. Someone had to start out rapping slowly and carefully; you know like the rap that resembles the old-school style. After that, rap could start to develop gradually. For me, I feel like now in 2013, is like the year 1996 in American hip-hop. That's also how I choose my music. . . . I don't want to jump ahead and do something that the Egyptian audience isn't ready for.*[10]

Takki's "theory," and his attempt to tell the stories of both American and Egyptian hip-hop, illustrate yet another artistic narrative of origin.[11] According to Takki, Egyptian hip-hop is less developed, both temporally and substantially, than American hip-hop; the Egyptian public is not ready for this form of cultural expression. What Takki did not reveal in his narrative was how Egyptian hip-hop, including his own music, which often incorporates the use of humor and Arabic instruments and beats, is connected to other forms of Egyptian cultural expression.

Origins? Mikki's and Takki's narratives evidence contrasting conceptions of the "origins" of rap.[12] Their narratives are representative of how most rappers in the underground hip-hop scene attempt to understand

---

9 E-Money is a member of the Egyptian hip-hop group Arabian Knightz.
10 Interview with Takki, March 2013.
11 Of course his narrative of the origins of American hip-hop is also problematic.
12 There is also a very interesting narrative of the origins of "Arabic hip-hop"; many rappers attribute its emergence to rappers in North Africa, specifically Morocco. They give credit to North African rappers as the forerunners of Arabic hip-hop, saying that these rappers started sometime in the 1980s, at least 10 years before Egyptians started rapping. They generally posit that these rappers were most likely influenced by French rappers.

the type of art they produce; some think of it as "natural" to their culture and some consider it "artificial," something that must be *introduced*. In order to claim that rap is a "natural," thus an "authentic," form of expression, rappers focus on the historical significance of poetry in the Arab world. Mikki is not the only rapper to make the claim that combining poetry with rhythm is an Arab innovation; Arabian Knightz also have a strikingly similar intro song on their album *Uknighted State of Arabia*.[13] Takki's perception that Egyptian rappers have to introduce rap slowly and carefully into Egyptian culture shows that he considers rap as the very opposite of "natural;" rather, it is an "artificial" import and with time the public will get used to it. Other Egyptian hip-hop artists, such as the rapper Shobokshy, are on Takki's side; he views rap as a completely American product that started in the 1970s, and says that anyone who claims otherwise does not know anything about rap.[14] F Killa was also in agreement with Takki; he says that he does not understand how some Egyptian rappers consider themselves "real" rappers if they do not know the origins of the genre.[15] Rappers who use this narrative are also claiming authenticity in another way; they assert that by knowing the "real" history of rap, they have the right to use this form of expression, as they know where it comes from and they understand its history. A recent statement from Deeb exemplifies how rappers can simultaneously identify with American rappers and imply there is something very "natural" about rapping for Arabs. During a radio interview in New York in 2013, the host asked Deeb about the artists he listened to when he was growing up. Deeb responded, "I think Nas was a big brother to me, to a lot of hip-hop artists … he was very poetic in the way he writes, he has a lot of imagery, and that's what drew me because I'm an Arab, Arabs love poetry, we love the choice of words and metaphors and all that."[16] This statement shows how these categories are not always thought of

---

13 Actually, there is some controversy surrounding this narrative. There is speculation that Ahmad Mikki "stole" this story from a conversation he had with Rush from Arabian Knightz. According to Sphinx from Arabian Knightz, before Ahmad Mikki became a rapper, they were at a mutual friend's house when Mikki mentioned that he does not particularly care for Arabic rap. Rush countered with a statement that rap is "originally Arab" and told him the story that is now the intro of Mikki's debut album.
14 Interview with Shobokshy, February 2013.
15 Interview with F Killa, March 2013.
16 Deeb speaking about hip-hop and the Arab Spring with WNYC radio, March 2013.

as being mutually exclusive; while Deeb would identify the originators of hip-hop as American and references an iconic American rapper as a "mentor," he also thinks of it as a "natural" form of Arab expression.

While Arab rappers use narratives of origin either to claim they are taking part in a "traditional" Arab art form or to state that they are doing "real" rap, like the American rappers, I hope to draw attention to an aspect of this art form that they largely overlook. The remainder of this chapter will carefully examine how Egyptian hip-hop and other Egyptian cultural practices and products from the twentieth century intersect, and I argue that these continuities point to yet another, seemingly indirect influence to which rappers and scholars have not given proper consideration.

Oppositional Cultural Products in Times of Political and Social Upheaval

1919 Revolution. During the 1919 Revolution, when Egyptians demanded an end to British occupation, people used songs and chants in colloquial Arabic to critique and insult the regime. Egyptian protesters used jokes and humor in these songs, chants, and poems to critique power. Ziad Fahmy's research on popular culture from 1870 to 1919 reveals historical continuities in cultural expression throughout the twentieth and twenty-first centuries. Fahmy challenges existing historiography on the 1919 Revolution by claiming that ordinary Egyptians, not elites, constructed a new national modern identity through media and popular culture. He studies plays, poetry, songs, newspapers, and jokes and discusses how humor and poetry played a role in resisting British colonialism (2011:xxi). He argues that "ordinary" Egyptians resisted different forms of domination during this time period through a variety of cultural products (2011:18). Aside from being entertaining, these forms "offered a highly accessible creative outlet for national discussions and even sociopolitical resistance" (2011:19).

Humor is also a critical component of Egyptian underground hip-hop. I would argue that Egyptian hip-hop, in its blending of humor and critique, served the same purpose during the January 25 Revolution, and arguably even earlier. Some rappers skillfully interweave multiple layers of meaning to express their views while also drawing attention to their lyrical abilities. The Egyptian rapper Shobokshy uses humor to comment on a certain presidential candidate in the 2012 election:

He's useless.
*******, the shoe symbol.
Adidas or Nike? No, it's a Crisis!
Where's the flip-flop? Didn't they say "it was lost"?[17]
Whether it's a shoe or a flip-flop, you can wear it anyway.

This is the chorus of the song titled "Sons of Bitches."[18] Shobokshy begins by telling his listeners, "I don't usually curse, but this time I'm speaking on behalf of all the revolutionaries." Thus the severity of the situation has pushed him to an "improper" mode of behavior. Every presidential candidate had to choose a symbol for the voting process; Shobokshy curses this candidate by referring to his symbol as a shoe (calling someone a shoe in Egypt is an insult) rather than his actual symbol. He takes the joke a step further by naming different popular brands of shoes and states that the brand of this candidate's shoe is "Crisis."

In addition to the use of humor, Fahmy also examines the relationship between cultural products and politics. He explores how cultural workers during the 1919 Revolution used colloquial songs and poetry in an attempt to "motivate mass action through appeals to the listeners' and readers' patriotic sentiments" (2011:156). Fahmy discusses how people distributed pamphlets and leaflets of songs and chants; "the words they contained were meant to be read aloud or performed" (2011:156). Similarly, prior to, during, and following the January 25 Revolution, Egyptian hip-hop artists sought to distribute and circulate their revolutionary ideas as well. This distribution came in a variety of forms, such as Facebook and YouTube. However, some hip-hop artists adopted some of the "old-school" methods of circulation; they spread their ideas and messages by going to the square and performing or writing chants. The two rappers Rush, from the hip-hop group Arabian Knightz, and Deeb both claim they helped people write chants during the

---

17 This is a reference to a popular *sha'bi* song titled "Fuck, I Lost My Flip-flop." This is further proof of the nuanced elements and influences that comprise Egyptian underground hip-hop music.

18 The title of the song is actually "Wilad mirat al-asad," which would translate to 'The Children of the Lioness'; instead of the term *labwa* ('lioness'), he uses *mirat al-asad* ('the lion's wife'). As *labwa* is the Egyptian colloquial equivalent of 'bitch,' he chooses to use more "polite" language that possesses the same meaning; still, his intention was to call that person a son of a bitch. He told me he thought this was a funny and clever way of conveying his message.

Oppositional Cultural Products 27

revolution. Furthermore, other "ordinary Egyptians" took excerpts from hip-hop songs and actually wrote them on posters as a way to express their continued discontent with the political situation after the revolution. For example, the lyrics of the Egyptian underground hip-hop song, "Who's the Target?" were written by a protester as a way to speak against the control of the Supreme Council of the Armed Forces (SCAF):

> *Who's the target? Me, my religion, or my country?*
> *My mother, my sister, or my children?*
> *I'm calling out in the loudest voice I have, I'm calling out,*
> *I'm telling you that you have no right to enslave me.*

Three hip-hop artists released "Who's the Target?" in December 2011.[19] They address a variety of issues ranging from pornography to Palestine. The protesters in figure 1 used these words to articulate their critiques of SCAF, showing how lyrics often transcend both artistic intention and temporal constraints. Oppositional cultural products have a life of their own, which Egyptians recycle and remake to contest new forms of oppression.

Mounah Khouri's work also draws attention to the long history of Egyptian poetry as a site of critique of occupation and freedom (1971:14).

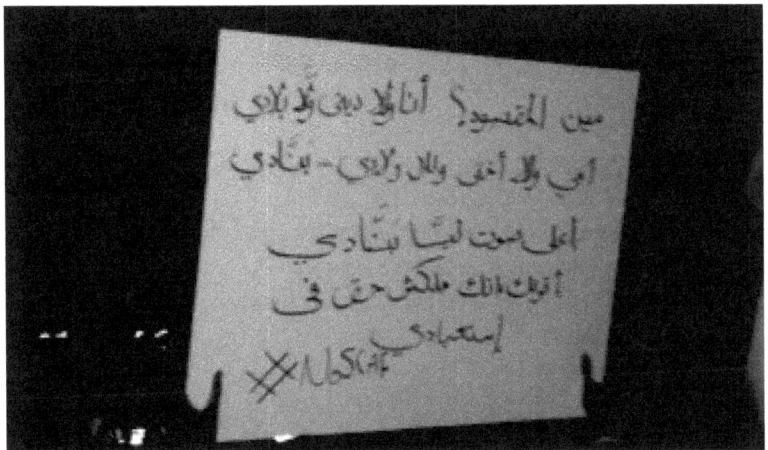

Fig. 1. "Who's the Target?" anti-SCAF protest banner

---

19 The artists released the song on YouTube in 2011; however, the writers told me they wrote parts of this song nearly six years ago and performed it prior to this date.

She examines the poetry leading up to and during the 1919 Revolution to discuss how people used poetry to protest and resist. The correlation between the street poetry of the 1919 Revolution and the hip-hop of today (which also often comes in the form of street poetry) is a difficult, and even problematic, one to trace. Most of my interlocutors were not aware of the striking similarities between some of the chants from this earlier historical period and the chants/raps they created during their time in Tahrir Square. However, there are many significant interactions between earlier forms and contemporary uses of poetry, again showing how words and art have their own lives.

Examining the poems of the Egyptian cultural icon Sayyid Darwish and the rapper Deeb reveals how contemporary Egyptian cultural workers are drawing on a deep cultural repository. Fahmy speaks of Sayyid Darwish's song "Stand Up, Egyptian" ("Um ya Masri") and discusses an intelligence report[20] on the Egyptian situation from 1919 that claimed authorities found a song in Port Said that was encouraging lazy Egyptians to start being more patriotic (Fahmy 2011:157). He argues that the report was most probably referring to Darwish's song:

Stand up, Egyptian!
Egypt always calls for you.
Lead me to victory.
My triumph is a debt you must repay.
The day that my happiness was needlessly taken away right before
    your eyes,
Restore my glory, the glory which you wasted away.

Deeb, the rapper I discussed at the beginning of this chapter, released a song with the same title after the revolution in order to encourage Egyptians to continue with the revolution. This is his version of the song:

Stand up, Egyptian!
Revolutions don't finish in a day and a night.
Try harder, hold on, get a grip.

---

20 Fahmy cites this intelligence report in *Ordinary Egyptians* (2011): "Intelligence Report on the Egyptian Situation," July 15, 1919, Great Britain, Public Records Office, FO 141/781/8915.

Don't worry about the "production wheel."
The revolution must come from within.
Tomorrow is better than before.

Deeb says he originally wrote these lines as a poem to express his feelings when Mubarak stepped down. When he transformed his poem into a song, he hoped to remind people that revolution is "a way of life"[21] and that real social and political change takes time. A Lebanese rapper[22] encouraged him to use Sayyid Darwish's version as the sample. While Deeb did not consider Darwish's version of the song while he was writing his, it is interesting to consider how both versions seek to encourage resistance, motivate the masses, and remind people of their responsibility in securing a better future. Deeb may not have consciously considered Darwish's version; however it was probably stored in his archive of 'cultural memory.' The presence of Egyptian popular culture in aspects of daily life and the reinforcement of the importance of certain cultural icons contribute to this archive. Furthermore, this archive of cultural memory extends to the broader Arab world. The Lebanese rapper's familiarity with Darwish's work shows how cultural icons from Egypt are also known throughout the Arab world, forming part of a collective cultural memory.

Cultural opposition of the 1950s, 1960s, and 1970s. Some of the most influential artists who have used music and poetry as a form of opposition are Ahmad Fu'ad Nigm (1929–2013), Salah Jahin (1930–1986), and 'Abd al-Rahman al-Abnudi (1938–2015). Ahmad Fu'ad Nigm, who wrote poetic lyrics for the famous Shaykh Imam, is known for his "social comment on the corruption of official life" (Hindi 1979:50). This is a critical example of the formative dialectic between art and politics. Some of my interlocutors identify with this generation of artists and refer to them as important influences. Others say they have never listened to these artists and do not feel there is a connection between this form of cultural expression and their music. Nigm's poetry focuses on political corruption, and some of my interlocutors understand this work as a "tradition" that they are continuing in their own work. Indeed, one rapper argued that hip-hop is now the *only* appropriate musical genre to express social and political critique.

---

21 MIX FM Saudi Arabia, "Why Hip-Hop?," December 8, 2011.
22 Edd Abbas from the Lebanese hip-hop group Fareeq el Altrash.

In his book *The Study of the Vernacular Poetry of Ahmad Fu'ad Nigm*, Kamal Abdel-Malek says that one should not "assume that Nigm's revolutionary *azgal*[23] with their sharp ends and political venom are something new" (1990:5). He goes on to briefly trace other events in Egypt's history in which colloquial poets resisted and critiqued hegemonic powers. Abdel-Malek reminds us that these sorts of cultural products have long historical trajectories and genealogies as forms of both political and aesthetic expression. Reem Saad's article, "The Egyptian Revolution: A Triumph of Poetry," also draws attention to how people referenced poetry in newspaper articles and through social media during the eleven days between the ouster of former Tunisian president Ben Ali and the start of the January 25 Revolution in Egypt (2012:63). Saad points to the way in which people during this time were drawing inspiration from Nigm's revolutionary poetry that he wrote in the late 1970s (Saad 2012:64). Thus, the writers, journalists, and ordinary people who referenced Nigm's words over 30 years later were also drawing from their archives of cultural memory in similar ways to some of the Egyptian rappers I discuss. This is further evidence of the fact that cultural products have unique "lives" and their power and validity are not constrained to a single point in history.

Another important figure is Salah Jahin, who was known as the poet of the 1952 Revolution; his poetry reflects the inspiration he drew from this event (Armbrust 1996:60). Jahin wrote in colloquial Arabic and often in the first person, giving his listener and reader "a feel of proximity and tangibility both physically and emotionally" (Radwan 2012:118). Additionally, his poems were often full of political and social criticism (Radwan 2012:119). The use of the first person is especially interesting, as this is a technique many of the rappers use to create intimacy with their audiences. Few of my interlocutors claim Jahin as an influence, but most of them are deeply familiar with his work and identify him as an important Egyptian cultural icon. I suspect they may have been indirectly influenced, as Jahin's nationalist songs were popular and widespread and other artists started to follow his lead and use the first-person technique. Here is an example of this technique in Jahin's poem, "My Heart Was a Rattle and Became a Bell":

---

23 Colloquial poetry.

*My heart was a rattle and became a bell.
I jingled it and the servants and guards woke up.
I am the clown . . . why did you get up and get frightened?
I don't have a sword in my hand and there is no horse under me.*

Aly Talibab's 2011 song "Perfection" shows how the use of the first person can allow the artist to situate himself within the broader social and political climate that surrounds him. While it is clear that Talibab is commenting on society, by using the first person he also places himself within society—he is part of both the problem and the potential solution. He addresses his internal conflict of feeling helpless and empowered at once:

*I am the paralyzed.
I am the one with the loud voice.
I am the one demanding democracy
And I take my rights with my arm.*

The following excerpt is from Cairokee and Zap Tharwat's 2012 song "Stand Your Ground," released one year after the revolution.[24] Zap's words embody the events of the revolution. He interweaves personal and collective experience.

*I am those who died a year ago
. . . the killer who wasn't hanged.
I am the words on the paper.
I am the one who is burned from inside.
I am the one whose hair turned gray when the student died.
I am the one standing my ground no matter what they say or how
    brutal they are.*

All three excerpts represent the subjective and the collective, the personal and the political, and the real and the metaphorical. The use of the first person allows each of the artists to simultaneously position himself as one of the people and share his own personal opinions and experiences. There are interesting similarities between Jahin's poem and Talibab's. Jahin expresses the transition of his heart from a rattle to a

---
24 Zap wrote this verse for Cairokee's song.

bell; his calls for change became louder. Talibab's first two lines discuss inability and action; he juxtaposes the people who cannot do anything with the people who can. Jahin's and Talibab's statements represent contrasts and transitions—weakness and courage, stasis and urgency. Both seem to be speaking of an individual and social awakening. Zap's verse starts by positioning himself in the collective; he represents everyone or anyone—the good and the bad, the innocent and the guilty. The tone takes a more personal turn by the last line when it becomes clear he is locating his social role as a revolutionary and a fighter. By providing their listeners with the possibility of locating themselves within them, all three verses allow the listeners to form connections with the words and the artists.

Another forefather of colloquial poetry, 'Abd al-Rahman al-Abnudi, has had more of a direct influence on some of my interlocutors. Major cultural icons such as 'Abd al-Halim Hafiz, Shadia, and Muhammad Munir have popularized his poetry. Some hip-hop artists have informed me that prior to the revolution they adopted his techniques of using specific imagery to elicit emotion and evoking metaphors to mask the true subject of their songs. In fact, an underground Egyptian band (Cairokee)[25] asked al-Abnudi if they could turn his poem "We Are the People" into a song. Al-Abnudi wrote the song nearly 30 years ago; however, these artists felt the lyrics appropriately expressed the messages they are trying to deliver through their music. This is the first verse of "We Are the People":

From every direction of the muted cities
Thousands of youth, crawling,
Calling out for the death of the dawn.
They waited dawn after dawn
For the killing to stop
Or the fist to unclench,
So they left,
Demanding the arrest of the fist and a helping hand.

---

25 Cairokee is an underground rock band in Egypt. While Cairokee does not make hip-hop music, they often collaborate with a popular underground hip-hop artist, Zap Tharwat. The underground hip-hop scene in Egypt is most certainly part of the broader underground scene and these artists often address similar issues.

Fig. 2. Two poets: Ahmed (Zap) Tharwat and 'Abd al-Rahman al-Abnudi

Al-Abnundi's "fist" is obviously a metaphor for the government. The words resonate today just as they did 30 years ago.

Zap Tharwat,[26] the rapper discussed above, had the opportunity to meet with al-Abnudi when the lead singer from Cairokee went to visit him at his home in Ismailiya to discuss the poem/song "We Are the People." Zap asked if he could join, as he has always respected al-Abnudi's work. Zap was pleasantly surprised when al-Abnudi complimented him on his verse in "Stand Your Ground" and his song "Good Morning," which begins: "I'm here to add to the words of Barghuti;[27] Egypt, we're almost there, please ... Let's bear with it" (Tharwat 2012:23). Zap never expected the poet to know anything about his work. He told me he spent the entire two hours at al-Abnudi's house in disbelief. He learned that the poet values poetry more than anything else in life; he told Zap that he would die without it. A week later, al-Abnudi called to ask if Zap would come again because he wanted to use his voice to record one of his poems.

---

26 Zap Tharwat is a poet as well as a rapper. He published two books of poetry in 2012, titled *Agenda: Poetic Attempts* and *Peace*.

27 The poet Tamim Barghouti, son of the Palestinian poet Mourid Barghouti and the Egyptian writer Radwa Ashour.

Thus through this cross-generational exchange these artists were able to engage, build on, and respond to each other's work, further demonstrating how cultural products have their own lives, which often lack temporal constraints.

Conclusion

This chapter has explored the more political hip-hop that artists from the Egyptian underground hip-hop scene produce. It is not all political and it is not always centered on revolutionary ideas and protest; Egyptian hip-hop existed more than 10 years prior to the revolution and contains diverse themes. I focus on the revolution here only to draw attention to the continuities in Egyptian cultural products from times of political upheaval. By analyzing the continuities in the types of music and poetry that cultural workers produced during these specific moments in Egypt's history, we can see that major events tend to inspire the outpouring of products with commonalities; however, these commonalities emerge in new and nuanced forms of expression. Both a synchronic and a diachronic analysis will lead to a better understanding of the creation of cultural products.

Locating Egyptian hip-hop in other forms of cultural expression in Egypt is not to deny the influence of Western hip-hop artists. In fact, almost every rapper I have spoken with lists the names of major American rappers as some of their greatest influences and inspiration, usually following life, the streets, and God. While these rappers listen to and respect the music of some American rappers, they do not mimic this form of hip-hop. Music moves through space and time in a variety of ways; it is useful not to limit our analysis of music to localization and appropriation. Furthermore, cultural products have their own histories; the relevance of music, art, and poetry is not confined to a specific period of time. Additionally, Egyptian rappers are drawing on archives of cultural memory, and this most certainly influences their work. Hip-hop is by no means a monolithic category; it has multiple layers and comes in a variety of packages. Taste, commodification, and values of the field all contribute to the differences and specificities in the music.

CHAPTER 3

Degrees of Opposition: Hip-Hop and Expression

"It's not just hip-hop, it's a movement." Arabian Knightz[1]

Using hip-hop as a medium of opposition is not a new phenomenon; it has its own history. Despite the fact that the genre is now highly commercialized and commodified in various ways and places, many artists around the world still use it as a tool to speak against oppression. Most Egyptian underground hip-hop artists express opposition to hegemonic structures through their music. Rap acts as a multi-layered form of expression and Egyptian rappers negotiate and articulate their disapproval of these structures in a variety of ways. While political opposition is a prominent theme in the artists' lyrics, various political entities are not the sole structures that these rappers are against. Their music evidences multifaceted opposition that reflects their dissatisfaction with mainstream forms of popular culture; social circumstances in their country and the Arab region; local and international powers; and governmental entities. Thus, it is useful to view Egyptian hip-hop as a movement—a movement that seeks to create new realities and imagine how things *could* be. Egyptian rappers offer their audience alternatives; they encourage their listeners to recognize the realities of their societies and to imagine new social, cultural, political, and economic possibilities.

This chapter examines music from the Egyptian underground hip-hop scene to see how it operates as a site of struggle. How is Egyptian hip-hop both determined by power structures and a site of contestation?

---

[1] This is a message all members of Arabian Knightz repeatedly emphasize through a number of mediums; it also appears on the back cover of their *Uknighted State of Arabia* CD insert.

What can this music tell us about the inextricable relationship between culture and power? What exactly do Egyptian rappers oppose? How does this opposition reflect dominant ideology? How do their oppositional ideas and lyrics shift when market forces intervene?

In this chapter we will see how oppositional discourse concerning issues such as unemployment, sexual harassment, and poverty is actually imbued with hegemonic ideology and reinforces dominant cultural stereotypes and assumptions.

Habibi Music

The opposition to mainstream cultural products is one primary form of expression of dissatisfaction with dominant cultural trends. Throughout the course of my fieldwork, rappers repeatedly referred to what they call *habibi* music. *Habibi* music is mainstream Arabic pop, which mostly focuses on romantic love and dominates Egypt's mainstream music scene. Hip-hop artists often complained about how the majority of Egyptians waste their time listening to this music, which they described as full of empty, idealized, and romantic stories. Egyptian underground rappers seek to offer an alternative to *habibi* music; they hope to create music that will inspire thought and action. This is much in line with the goal of hip-hop artists around the globe: artists seek to create meaningful lyrics that will lead to critical thought and consideration of their messages. My interlocutors stated that hip-hop is a medium that can deliver important messages and address social and political problems. The rapper Rush from Arabian Knightz expressed his disapproval of the mass consumption of *habibi* music: "We have a lot of problems that are not about 'how she left me' and 'oh she loves me.' We have bigger issues to care about right now, especially our generation."[2] Rush emphasizes the need for a more conscious form of music; he believes society should be addressing its problems through music rather than attempting to escape them. However, some rappers posit that the purpose of this music is to express individual and collective feelings; they were not completely opposed to the occasional love-themed rap song. Ibrahim Farouk from Asfalt said that "you are supposed to express people's feelings, and love and relationships are part of this . . . as long as you don't make an entire album about love."[3] When I

---

2 Rush speaking on an unreleased documentary, "Lyrics Revolt," by Torath Production.
3 Interview with Ibrahim Farouk, May 2012.

asked F Killa about rappers writing love songs he said that "[rappers] are supposed to write about whatever they are feeling at that time," thus the occasional love song is not a problem. For most rappers, it seems there is a fine line between *habibi* music, which expresses "empty" romance, and a love-themed rap song, which expresses people's "real" feelings.

Most Egyptian hip-hop songs I have listened to inherently oppose *habibi* music by discussing issues centered on their aim to raise social awareness.[4] There are also songs that directly attack this genre. Direct opposition to *habibi* music is highlighted here in the following lines from Abyusif's[5] "A French Song" (2007), in which he expresses how he feels about singing about love.

I won't sing for love,
I won't even think about it.
They come to me and they stop.
Consider me a filter.

Abyusif asserts that even when ideas for love songs approach him or start to enter his mind, he filters them out. For Abyusif it is pointless to engage this type of music; for him, love is not a legitimate topic to approach in hip-hop.

Ibrahim Farouk and Deeb wrote the following verse in 2006.[6] It critiques another aspect of *habibi* music—the scantily dressed pop stars who accompany the music in videos. This verse shows that the artists consider the music's content pointless and the videos as a source of distraction from productive activities.

---

4   I am generalizing here. I have surveyed over 300 songs and the *majority* of them deal with political and social issues. However, there are songs dealing with values important to the underground rap scene in Egypt, such as flow and creativity, and in line with this there are some dis-tracks in which rappers comment on each other's skills. Additionally, there are two songs that come to mind that express the themes of *habibi* music—the rapper Sony has a song titled "I'm Single" and Takki has a song called "This Girl Is a Rocket."

5   This is his "rap name"; it is pronounced "Abusive," which is a play on his given name, Youssef Altay.

6   The song title is "al-'Ebara fi al-'abara." The explanation that its translation would require (considering the artists' intentions and play on words as they explained to me) is too complicated to include here.

> *Substances have taken over our brains*
> *And everyone bought a satellite dish.*
> *They watch Melody and Mazzika.*[7]
> *I say, "Excuse me,*
> *Come on, people, enough of these channels!*
> *All the videos have become full of nude scenes,*
> *From 'Bossy Samir' to 'Dolly' to what's-her-name.*
> *Man, please change the channel to the economic news."*

Ibrahim and Deeb are calling for people to stop filling their minds with the overly sexualized images of female pop stars and to spend their time paying attention to some of the more important issues, such as keeping up with the economy.

Artists in the hip-hop movement in Egypt are concerned with creating a more socially and politically conscious form of music. They perceive Arabic pop music as an escape, a distraction, and an unhealthy refuge that allows people to ignore the real problems they face. Thus, Egyptian rappers seek to open discussions concerning social issues through their music. They are actively forming and producing a new cultural product to expand options for consumers of these forms of popular culture.

"Rapping about Our Problems": Social Concerns

Keeping in mind Rush's statement that "we have a lot of problems," I examine what the Egyptian rappers perceive as their problems. We can view these concerns as the rappers' expression of opposition to practices of both "ordinary" people and the government. Most rappers in the underground Egyptian hip-hop scene make it a point to convey that they make music in order to discuss their own as well as society's problems. I focus on these artists' social concerns through their lyrics; here I examine songs specifically addressing unemployment, slums, sexual harassment, and drugs. The songs also draw attention to education, religious discrimination, gender roles, and the broader economic issues that permeate Egyptian

---

[7] Melody and Mazzika are television channels that air music videos featuring Arab pop stars and *habibi* music.

society.[8] The lyrics in these songs exemplify nuanced alternative realities in which the artists either directly or subtly imagine future possibilities.

Unemployment. "Guys at Cafés," a song Asfalt[9] wrote in 2009, addresses unemployment as a social issue that leads to crowded streets and men being forced into doing "women's work" in order to survive. The artists also hint at the various forms of corruption within the dynamics of the workforce.

You have to fill up your résumé to the fullest extent,
Mention that you even have magician skills.
The workforce is all dependent on connections.
Unemployment made our streets crowded.
Isn't it wrong that men started to do women's work?
Look at the guys at the cafés,
Sitting around, not finding work, and they don't even intend to.
Whoever is still looking is called relentless.
Everybody get up, enough complaints!
Since I was a child, my father said, "Study and you will learn."
But he never told me that work requires connections.
Look at the guys, smoking day and night.
Where should we look, man, we've become a lazy generation.
Useless generation, there's no work for us, who's with me?
Any job opportunity vanishes in front of my eyes.
Poor people, victims, deducted salaries—
They are all trying to make a living inside the government's land.

The artists use humor[10] to discuss the devastating problem of unemployment in Egypt. From the start of the song, these rappers emphasize

---

8   I have selected songs that I feel are representative of the social concerns Egyptian rappers generally address. However, I have heard other songs that address issues of poverty, racism, sectarianism, and women's rights. Including them all is beyond the scope of this chapter.

9   Both members of Asfalt were college graduates. At the time of this research, one was unemployed and the other was working for a minimal income at a call center. The topic of this song was certainly inspired by personal experience.

10 See chapter two for a more in-depth discussion on the use of humor in Egyptian hip-hop.

that securing work in Egypt is not based on qualifications. In the first line of the song the artists rap, "Wanted: girl to work, with experience, being pretty is a must and she should know how to sweet-talk." For women, "qualifications" simply means being beautiful and sweet. For men, it is more complicated. The artists stress that people do not obtain work based on their qualifications and education, but rather on whom they know. Lines such as "The whole workforce is dependent on connections" and "[My father] never told me that work requires connections" reveal the concern that the whole employment system is corrupt.

Additionally, throughout the song the artists simultaneously express a dual opposition; they are both blaming the government and shaming the people for their roles in this problem. The lines "Until the public sector privatized the whole market" and "They are all trying to make a living in the government's land" show that the artists view the government as a major factor in national unemployment. However, other lines suggest that the rappers also perceive the *people* as the heart of the problem. They refer to their generation as "useless" and paint a picture of lazy men lounging their lives away, "smoking day and night." These rappers imply that "guys" are sitting around at cafés not just because they have nothing else to do, but because they have no intention of securing work or making a real effort to find a job. By stating "we've become a lazy generation," the artists attribute the problem of unemployment to popular attitudes. The song ends on an optimistic note with "For your information, we don't believe in the impossible! Without us who's going to continue the civilization of the Nile Valley?" Suggesting the possibility of change and a better future is one way artists express an alternate reality. The correlation between the present and the ancient past is one way to narrate an Egyptian society that has the responsibility and potential to carry on a great "civilization." At the same time, and despite the rhetoric of opposition, these artists reify gendered notions of "women's" work as well as depictions of the people as lazy.

Poverty. The issues of poverty and poor living conditions occupy many rappers. EL Zero, F Killa, MC Monadel, and Mr. Kordy collaborated on a song about the slums of Cairo and the problems that the people in these "informal" areas face. This is EL Zero's verse from the 2010 song "Slums":

> *Please God, bless us with peace.*
> *I heard the streets talking.*
> *Everybody is saying "slums."*
> *Not clear and unseen,*
> *Barbaric, can't see them or feel them.*
> *Get closer to them and try to know the truth from them.*
> *You will find them to be simple people.*
> *[They are] unseen on the map.*
> *They will say "God made us like that";*
> *"Some are rich and some are poor."*
> *We see a lot of people but in different places.*
> *He lives in the projects, right inside the slums.*
> *Poor people, gang wars.*

The rappers who wrote "Slums" attempt to provide their listening audience with a glimpse of the lives of the people who live in these areas. However, the perspective they provide is of an outsider looking in; none of these rappers come from the slums of which they speak.[11] The entire song uses the pronouns "they," "he," and "she." There are no references in which the rappers use "we" to refer to collective experience. These artists make it very clear that they are not from these slums. However, they do feel it necessary to inform their listeners of the reality of people living there. They assume their listeners know nothing of this world and encourage them to take a closer look. This shows that the rappers are positioning themselves as distinct from "ordinary" people; they can traverse various worlds and educate others on their findings.

From the song, the listener gets the sense that these slums exist in some secret and hidden world where "simple" people live unfortunate lives in despair. The chorus goes on to say that in the slums children are forced to eat trash and inhabitants accept their circumstances as part of God's plan. In the last line of the chorus, the rappers go as far as posing the question, "Why are these people like that?" While this song shows the rappers' sympathy with anyone who lives a life of poverty, deprivation, and humility, it is also imbued with dominant stereotypical notions of the poor. Despite their claims to oppositional culture, then,

---

11 El-Zero, who wrote this verse, is from a pretty typically middle-class Egyptian home.

the rappers reinforce the dominant and mainstream ideology of some causal relationship between poverty and ignorance.

The rappers bring the slum experience to light and place it among other social concerns of which they feel Egyptian society should be aware. Additionally, in the chorus, the rappers say that "it's impossible that life stays like that," which directs attention to the alternative—that life does *not* continue on in the same way for the inhabitants of the slums. This song, just as we saw in "Guys at Cafés," encourages people to imagine that conditions could improve. The performers could even be proposing that people ask themselves how they could play a role in this possibility for change. However, they propose this possibility to people who listen to their music—not the poor themselves. Thus, it is not the poor but the audience that have the capability to inspire change.

Sexual harassment. Another social concern is the increased occurrence of sexual harassment in recent years. Since the January 25 Revolution there have been several accounts of brutal attacks on women in public spaces, such as in the streets and at protest gatherings. These attacks threaten women's security and often deter women from participating in protests. In response to this problem, several initiatives have started to battle sexual harassment.[12] Rappers in the underground scene are also battling this issue with their music. F Killa released a song in 2012 titled "A Message to Every Harasser." He released it prior to the United Nations International Women's Day and performed the song at the Women's Day event, which called for an end to violence against women. F Killa's song uses a shaming technique in which the rapper directly addresses the harassers. While the writer cannot relate to a woman's feelings when she experiences this type of harassment, he can appeal to men's social and moral values. This is the first verse and chorus of F Killa's song addressing all the sexual harassers in Egypt:

She went down to participate,
To express her anger in [Tahrir] Square.
Anger flipped to harassment from some animals.
During the chaos they reached for every place of her body.
It's not her fault; it's the fault of the undignified community.

---

12   Harassmap and No to Harassment (*La li-l taharush*) are a few of these initiatives.

> We took the number two ranking and silver medal in harassing women.
> It's obvious to the world that we are sexually deprived.
> Congratulations, Egyptians, you lost your prestige and essence;
> In a day and a night you reversed our old reputation.
> They used us as examples back in the day.
> Our country represented safety and human respect,
> Sacred places, no religious discrimination.
> Enough shame!
> Three-quarters of our youth are suffering from addiction.
> What's the point of harassing a girl until it becomes a habit?
> And it grows over time. Where's your manhood and your willpower?
> We never behaved like that, gentlemen!
> A message for every harasser: it's time for extermination!

F Killa shames his fellow Egyptians by calling attention to "Egypt's reputation." He is asking people to imagine how Egypt appears to the rest of the world. He evokes a time in Egypt's past when he claims it was known for its "safety," "human respect," and lack of "religious discrimination." Now Egypt has the "silver medal" in harassment. While F Killa does not seem to directly blame any "powers from above" for this problem, he situates the incident at a protest in Tahrir Square, which directly corresponds to the political upheaval in the country. The girl would have never had to go to Tahrir Square, where "they reached for every place of her body," had she not been angry, and we assume this anger came from the political circumstances in her country. But while F Killa does not directly say that the girl in his song should not have been in Tahrir, it also seems that through his lyrics he tells a story, which would incite fear in any woman to participate in public gatherings.

While F Killa's song draws attention to this serious issue, which he supposedly opposes, it simultaneously reinforces dominant patriarchal attitudes. The whole tone of the verse places the entire reputation of a country in the hands of men. He refers to "our reputation," and says "they used *us* as examples back in the day." As the song is directed toward men, he certainly uses "us" to refer to himself and the rest of the male population. Furthermore, when he congratulates Egyptians for throwing away their "prestige," he seems to be saying that men carry the responsibility of maintaining social values.

Egyptian rap documents social and political events as they occur, and so it was not surprising that F Killa, along with other rappers, released songs discussing sexual harassment. During a discussion with F Killa, he provided me with his position on harassment.

> *I can verbally harass a girl, no problem, but in terms of sexual harassment, no, no way. You know there is a difference between verbal harassment when you say something nice to a girl . . . it has its limits, and sexual harassment when you touch a girl. . . . People think because there is no government, or no security, that they can sexually harass any girl in the street. . . . People say that my personality is the complete opposite of the song. But I wrote about what I saw and what I felt at that moment. This is how rap is.*[13]

A video of a girl being violently harassed in Tahrir Square pushed F Killa to consider a social issue to which he had not previously given much thought. He struggles to justify his position as a self-admitted verbal harasser. However, the experience of watching this horrible act allowed him to formulate a clear opinion on the issue and create an imagined world in which harassers are "exterminated," "beaten," "humiliated," and may even have their "hand cut off."[14] It also seems he is calling for a return to a previous era in which Egyptian men were "gentlemen" and imagines how Egyptian society could be without this problem. However, he places the responsibility of these changes in the hands of men, and in some notion of gentlemanly "tradition." Ultimately, his call for change reinforces patriarchal ideology. Furthermore, it may be important to question F Killa's motivation in writing this song. Seemingly, oppositional rap is not necessarily oppositional—rappers also follow trends, which may lead to the accumulation of greater recognition. Additionally, 'oppositional rap' sometimes reinforces and even encourages dominant attitudes concerning gender roles. In this sense, it is useful to understand that there are many layers to opposition, and sometimes rappers only touch on the surface layer.

---

13 Interview with F Killa, April 2013.
14 These quotes come from the chorus, which is not provided here.

"Rapping about Our Problems": Social Concerns

Drugs. As F Killa points out in "A Message to Every Harasser," drugs and addiction are part of the rappers' social concerns. Zap Tharwat raps about hashish in the song titled "How Many" from 2012. He raps from the perspective of the drug user, which is a technique many rappers use to create a certain intimacy and feeling of tangibility with the listeners.

> *They say whoever waits in patience every day will get what they want.*
> *I'm the one who's patient and know that I'm not responsible*
> *For choosing my time, for choosing my place,*
> *For choosing my name, or even for choosing the characteristics of my being.*
> *I said a lot of words to myself.*
> *Within the bounds of my imagination I will draw the best me and put on the nicest smile.*
> *But my imagination resists holding the pen*
> *To write, or draw, or to articulate my dreams.*
> *Bad circumstances and location affected the imagination.*
> *They made my imagination hollow, empty of any possibility.*
> *With smoking, I found the nicest comforts and an array of meanings;*
> *A lot of doors opened.*
> *But to be honest, I was afraid to lose the comfort I felt and the beautiful world I saw*
> *To go back to the old me that I hate.*
> *So I kept holding on to the cigarette, loving what's inside of it,*
> *And afterward, I got to know all the good things in life.*

Zap wrote this song "in the name of the people who do drugs and about the circumstances that make people smoke [hashish]."[15] He elaborated by indicating that the environment, or the conditions in Egypt, force people to escape through drug use. The only way to cope with their living conditions is to alter their state of consciousness; the only way to enjoy life is to find an alternate reality. He asserts that people who use drugs do so in order to find a sense of comfort and that once they find it, they do not want to return to the way life feels without drugs. This song

---
15 Conversation with Ahmed Tharwat, March 2013.

calls for people to face reality and find a way to accomplish dreams and inspire others through their strength, patience, and persistence.

These examples show how rappers are calling for two kinds of social change—structural and cultural. According to the rappers, if the conditions were better no one would have a reason to do drugs, slum dwellers would not be subject to miserable destinies, girls would not have to put themselves in situations in which they are harassed, and everyone would have an appropriate job according to their qualifications. There is an underlying critique of the government here. However, these rappers do not entirely blame some power structure from above for Egypt's problems; they also point to "ordinary" people as part of the problem. By calling on people to attend to these issues, these artists posit that they are *opposed to* or *in disagreement with* how things are. At the same time, they want their listeners to imagine the possibility that the circumstances do not have to be like this. Their message seems to be: we have the ability to change. Of course, while rappers promote the possibility of change for social conditions, they also aggressively demand change of political conditions. I address their opposition of political powers in the following section.

"The Powers That Be"

Sphinx:[16] *If we are all united, then* they *can't pick us off one at a time through wars and take out Iraq and Palestine. You know what I mean?*
Me: Who are they?
Sphinx: They *would be* the powers that be. *It could be considered the US, Israel, whatever, whatever people are holding power right now.*[17]

The rappers in the underground scene use their lyrics to speak against hegemonic powers. Their songs express opposition to international powers, primarily the US and Israel, as well as local powers. Opposition to international powers is primarily centered on issues concerning Palestine, such as the loss of historic Palestine and the Israeli state's continued confiscation of Palestinian land; its dispossession and brutalization of Palestinians;

---
16 Sphinx is a member of Arabian Knightz.
17 Interview with Sphinx, April 2012.

and the ongoing occupation. They also express skepticism that the US has any real interest in improving its dealings with the Arab world. Songs dealing with local powers address Mubarak's oppressive regime (mostly indirectly prior to the revolution). Following the revolution, artists have written songs criticizing the "transitional" rule of the Supreme Council of the Armed Forces (SCAF), the presidential candidates in the 2012 election, the Muslim Brotherhood, and Muhammad Morsi.

International powers. On the theme of opposition to international powers, the following song, "Obama," written by Zap Tharwat in 2009, expresses the artist's feelings about Obama's speech in June 2009 at Cairo University. This is the first verse:

Obama, they say he will erase the mark.[18]
We got into this vortex long time ago
And we shut up, we moved on.
We sprinkled flowers and flew pigeons for him.
Come on, Egypt, with the biggest and most beautiful smile.
People are silent, as if they are at dignity's funeral:
Shh shh, hush hush.
Obama is at the podium
Saying beautiful words.
Please, man, give us more!
He started with a greeting and peace:
"May peace be upon you, Arabs."
"The best people."
"I came to fool you, and say the same thing."
"I'll repeat history, like what they did before."
"Romans and Hyksos, Zionists and Americans."
"This is not the time for violence."
"I'm in a bad situation now and I have to be a coward."
"I'll con you again, as I'm the master of this place."

Zap sarcastically recounts Obama's speech. This verse expresses opposition to US policy in the Arab world. For Zap, the US government's intentions are the opposite of their promises regardless of who

---

18   Zap explained that the "mark" he is referring to is the bad reputation of the Arabs.

is president. Zap is simultaneously expressing his disapproval of the Arab people's willingness to accommodate the US president's visit, their eagerness to hear his empty promises, and their acceptance of a speech filled with lies. The verse paints a picture of people sitting on the edge of their seats, hanging on to every word of the newly elected president, and Zap is letting them know that they have been fooled.

The same song addresses Palestine in a later verse. He informs his listeners that the US government spent US$30 billion to help Israel build their military. For Zap, the relationship between the US and Israel is proof enough for why Arabs should not trust Obama. Israel is the other primary international power Egyptian rappers speak against. Palestine is a central topic in the underground hip-hop scene in Egypt and across the Arab world. In fact, some of my interlocutors have mentioned Palestinian rappers as sources of inspiration and influence.[19] Egyptian rappers create songs to show their solidarity with Palestinians and to express their deep concern with the brutality, wars, and occupation Palestinians face. There are dozens of songs concerning Palestine within the Egyptian underground scene,[20] most of them either address events as they occur, speak about the Palestinians' rights to their land, or focus on the multiple forms of oppression Palestinians experience on a daily basis. The following excerpt is particularly interesting because it expresses opposition to Israel by comparing the government's practices to the ultimate form of violence. It comes from a song called "I Want" by Asfalt. Ibrahim Farouk wrote this verse in 2009.

> *Violence is not hitting someone back,*
> *Violence is when you are paralyzed and someone is taking your land.*
> *Violence is when someone steals from your blessing and strips you of your decency,*
> *When it won't stop even if you beg for mercy and others are watching.*

---

19 Many of the rappers from the Palestinian rap scene started rapping before or around the same time as Egyptian rappers. DAM, the most prominent Palestinian rap group, started in 1999 and another group, Ramallah Underground, started in 2003.

20 I wish to stress the importance of this topic. The majority of rappers with whom I worked, or whose work I examined, have at least one song concerning Palestine; several of them have written three or four. Egyptian rappers often write lyrics dealing with oppression, and it is clear to them that Palestinians experience oppression on multiple levels, which explains the existence of so many songs on the topic.

> *Violence is people not living in peace; violence is going underground just to sleep.*
> *Violence isn't dissing someone in a song; violence isn't using weapons or calling your friends for backup;*
> *Violence is a country that has nuclear weapons and uses them every day even when there's an international ban.*
> *Some people are suffering from poverty; other people are using religion in war.*
> *Some people are living comfortably; other people are living in Palestine.*
> *Whoever said that violence is only razors and knives . . .*
> *Real violence isn't what you think it is.*

Ibrahim's verse deconstructs the commonly held notions of violence to show that Palestinians are experiencing what he refers to as "real violence." He asserts that living in Palestine is the very opposite of "living comfortably." Without ever naming Israel, nearly every line of this verse speaks directly against Israel's violent practices and policies, which strip Palestinians of their rights to live "in peace." Thus, Palestine emerges as the ultimate symbol of injustice.

Local powers. The rappers also use their lyrics to express their opposition to the Egyptian government. Prior to the January 25 Revolution, the lyrics against Egyptian political powers were primarily metaphorical. For example, in the song "Slums," which I discussed above, F Killa explained to me that he used his verse to speak against the regime in an indirect manner. His verse describes a girl who is suffering from poverty and lives a life of misery and despair. In the first few lines of his verse he raps, "The girl is chasing after food, she is following her role. She's carrying nine others on her back, may God be with her." He claims the "girl" he sings about is not just an average girl living in the slums: "People think I'm talking about a girl, but I meant something completely different . . . no one takes care of her . . . so if you focus you will notice that I'm trying to speak about the regime, but in a roundabout way."[21] F Killa asserts that the "girl" represents the starving Egyptian people, who carry the burden of the responsibilities the Egyptian government should be attending to.

---
21 Interview with F Killa, April 2013.

Others claim they also spoke about Mubarak and the regime through their music prior to the revolution, but generally they all say that their references were subtle or indirect due to fear of being arrested. However, there are a few examples of direct references to Mubarak and his family. These few lines come from MC Loser's 2008 song titled "Searching." The song has a highly sarcastic tone and the rapper expresses his opinion that nothing will change when people are scared to speak up.

We put an end to the politics by "cursing the president"?
A couple of words made me enthusiastic.
The economy is depleted and the money is in Jimmy's wallet!

In these lines MC Loser boldly asserts that simply cursing the president or saying a few critical words about him will not incite real change. By saying "a couple of words made me enthusiastic," MC Loser draws attention to his feeling that people were too easily excited by the slightest political critique. He is calling for people to speak up. In the meantime, while people continue to stay silent, Egypt's entire economy is in the hands of Mubarak's son Gamal, or "Jimmy."

These next lines come from the rapper Haty, in his 2007 song "Everything's Fine." This song describes Egypt as the very opposite of how he views it. Haty describes a society with no unemployment, a place where no one eats beans and everyone eats meat. In the middle of the song there is a slightly muted section:

Send a telegram to the president:
Tell him that everything is fine and the people are living carefree.

When Haty raps the word 'president' (*ra'is al-gumhuriya*), he plays with the sound so it is not completely clear what he is saying. Haty imagines an Egypt without Mubarak and raps about the conditions that could exist without an oppressive leader. Both Haty and MC Loser are calling for people to imagine an alternative in which there is no ruling family stealing from its people. They are posing the question: What would life be like without Mubarak?

Many songs that openly spoke against Mubarak and the regime were released by rappers during the revolution, and this form of direct, open opposition has continued in post-Mubarak Egypt. Specifically, Egyptian hip-hop artists express their opposition to Morsi and the Muslim Brothers. The following verses are from the song, "Hey, Morsi," from 2012. The rappers MC Amin, Sphinx, E-Money, and F Killa perform in the song. It explains why Morsi and the Brothers cannot be trusted and how they will inevitably carry on the Mubarak regime's practices. Before the first verse of the song, the rappers introduce themselves by rapping, "Sphinx . . . for president, E-Money . . . for president . . . F Killa . . . for president, MC Amin . . . for president, the Egyptian people . . . for president!"

> *For a long time we've been hearing about the Brothers,*
> *From Abdel Nasser and Sadat, from the devil Mubarak.*
> *We heard it everywhere.*
> *Shouts from Tahrir Square: "Never trust the Brothers!"*
> *Tell that to the prisoner.*
> *Your banned Brotherhood is moving the strings of the game.*
> *Your paid men do things blindly.*
> *You forgot when you used to be hiding in the holes?*
> *You came up, ate the revolution, and had the constitution as dessert!*
> *All you wanted was just the chair, why are you acting just like him?*
> *Shave your beard and you'll look just like Hosni.*

These rappers explicitly express their disapproval of the new president and the Muslim Brothers. By comparing Morsi to former president Mubarak (or the "devil"), they assert that nothing has changed and the new president is exactly like the old president—he just happens to have a beard, but is equally corrupt. For now, post–January 25 Egypt is a place in which rappers are willing to take risks and speak more freely.

In that spirit, rappers create new political imaginaries through their music. The following chorus and selected lines, from the 2013 Arabian Knightz song, "We Are the Government," exemplify this technique.

> *Starting today, there is no government;*
> *Starting today, we are the government.*

*We won't accept half of our freedom
And sell the rest.
I'm sure you saw before how our anger responds.*

Arabian Knightz express their opposition to all forms of government. They feel that the only way to gain real freedom is to take things into their own hands. They threaten that if they do not get what they want, they will demonstrate their anger again. This song represents a new vision; while it seems the majority of songs have an underlying tone of imagining a country with a new leader who will actually improve conditions, this song does not express that sentiment. Rather, it announces to the people that if *we* want to get things done, we have to do it ourselves, and we should not wait around for someone from above to implement change for us.

Out of all the political imaginaries I came across in the music I surveyed, the most fascinating had to be members of the Arab League who propose the USA—the United States of Arabia. Arabian Knightz[22]

Fig. 3. United States of Arabia t-shirt

---

22 Here it seems important to note that each member of Arabian Knightz spent some or all of their childhood outside of Egypt: Sphinx in the US, Rush in Oman, and Karim in Dubai. This may explain why, compared to the other rappers in the scene, they have the strongest connections with other rappers in the Arab world.

started this symbolic record label[23] to unite Arab hip-hop artists from around the world. It includes some Egyptian rappers such as F Killa and MC Amin, in addition to other prominent Arab artists such as Palestinian rapper Shadia Mansour, Syrian-American rapper Omar Offendum, Iraqi-Canadian rapper the Narcycist, and many more from around the Arab world. The members of the Arab League express their opposition to the "powers that be" and propose a united Arab world that has the potential to stand up against other international powers.

When I asked Sphinx about this idea of the USA, he said that he was very serious about this idea: "We want to unite the Arab world and finish what Abdel Nasser's idea was but just couldn't do it, so we wanna do it through the music to get the youth into it. If we want things to change it's not gonna happen in our lifetime. You know if Palestine was a state in the USA then it would be harder to mess with it because they would have the support of the other twenty-one states."[24] The rapper Rush raps about the idea of a united Arab world in the 2011 song "Arab World Unite," which features verses from eight other hip-hop artists from the region.

United States Arabia, twenty-two.
Break the chains that enslave us, twenty-two.
Fall like steel and stainless, bullet-proof.
Enough talk, let's see action.
Inch by inch, land by land, my country,
Person, person, individual, individual, my brothers.

It is clear that Egyptian rappers use their lyrics to express their dissatisfaction with and disapproval of various "powers that be." Moreover, this opposition sometimes expresses itself in proposals of alternative constructions of power relations. I will now examine how some rappers reject governmental entities' categorizations of cultural workers.

---

23 I refer to it as "symbolic" because as of now they do not actually produce records, although they hope to in the future.
24 Interview with Sphinx, March 2013. Sphinx was born in the US so our conversations were usually in English. His comments appear as he said them (in colloquial English).

"I'm Not a Monologist": Egyptian Rappers and the *Niqaba*

Egyptian rappers are oppositional in the sense that they defy musical categorization. That is, they are firmly outside of the canonical music scene in Egypt, at least officially. The Syndicate of Musicians, which my interlocutors simply refer to as the *naqaba*,[25] requires that any musician who performs[26] at venues be a cardholding member. The syndicate functions like a union; it recognizes artists and grants them specific rights, protections, and benefits in exchange for a yearly fee. It does not interfere with artistic production such as the lyrical content of the music. There is a separate government entity—called the *musanafat*[27]—that is responsible for reviewing and censoring all music that will be distributed or that is recorded with a record label.

Musicians who are not members and do not hold the official card of the *naqaba* are subject to fines. There is speculation whether the "fines" they are paying actually go to the syndicate or the individuals who approach the artists. There is no set fine and it is not based on a percentage of the income from performances or record sales. Ibrahim from the hip-hop duo Asfalt explained to me that the fine is negotiable: "Sometimes they ask for LE500 and we say no, so then they say, okay, 400, and in the end we pay 200 just so they go away. It's like when you go to the vegetable market and bargain for a kilo of tomatoes or something."[28] The artists say that they need to pay these people to make them go away so they can perform, even if they consider the money they are paying to be a bribe. This "fine" is most certainly a bribe, because it is the syndicate's responsibility to shut down any performances by musicians who are not members of the *naqaba*. I assume that the representatives of the syndicate who come to the performances go with the intention of collecting a bribe, rather than with the intention of shutting down the concert. Throughout the course of my fieldwork, I attended multiple concerts in which a *naqaba* representative showed up and demanded money before

---

25 *Naqaba* translates as 'syndicate'; the underground artists with whom I have spoken refer to the syndicate of musicians as "the Syndicate."
26 Regardless of whether they receive payment for their performance.
27 *Al-musanafat* is a state-controlled copyright authority which is responsible for filtering media output.
28 Conversation with Ibrahim Farouk, February 2013.

the performers went on stage. These representatives threatened to shut down the entire show if the musicians did not agree to pay the amount they demanded. However, I never attended a concert in which these representatives actually stopped the musicians from performing, which further supports the idea that their intent is to collect bribes.

Since the syndicate harasses Egyptian rappers because they are not cardholders, this seems like an easily resolvable problem. However, the act of becoming a syndicate member is not quite so simple for rappers. When musicians register with the *naqaba*, they must specify the category of music they produce and then they are tested to prove that they are real, talented musicians. The musicians must choose from a limited number of categories that the syndicate has set. There are a variety of categories for people who play musical instruments as well as those that specify the type of singer.[29] There is no category for a rapper or a hip-hop artist.[30] What the *naqaba* offers these artists is the ambiguous marker of "monologist." This does not satisfy the artists. Nearly every time I asked the artists about their syndicate membership, I received the same answer: "I am not a monologist."

Only one rapper in the underground scene is in fact—or at least according to the syndicate—a monologist. Takki, the sole rapper who holds the syndicate card, accepted this title because he signed a record deal in 2003 and needed it to perform. Takki is no longer in the mainstream music scene, and has returned to the underground scene where he enjoys more freedom in choosing the content of his music. Takki does not experience confrontations with the *naqaba*, but he does desire that they recognize hip-hop as a legitimate genre. This desire led him to create the Egyptian Hip-Hop union[31] in 2012. He believes that if all the hip-hop artists unite, people (specifically the syndicate) will be forced to recognize the prevalence of this genre in Egypt.[32] Nearly all of my interlocutors stated that what they hope for the future of hip-hop in

---

29 There is a category for *sha'bi* singer.
30 Interestingly, there is a category for a DJ. However, they are also not satisfied with this category as it simply specifies that they "play discs," and they believe this reduces the value of their work.
31 At this point in time, this is a purely symbolic union in the sense that it is not registered.
32 Conversation with Takki, February 2013.

Egypt is that it will reach a wider audience and become more popular. While Takki and some other artists are calling for the *naqaba* to create this category, rapper MC Amin is more skeptical. When I asked him about his experience with the *naqaba*, he informed me that he has not had any problems. I knew that the *naqaba* closely monitors these rappers' social media presence in order to attend concerts and collect fines, so I asked MC Amin why he thought he had not experienced any problems. He responded, "What can they do? When I have a concert and they come, all my friends are there. I refuse to pay and my friends are standing by my side so they leave. They don't frighten me." I asked him if he would like to join the syndicate if there was a fitting category and he responded, "I don't need to be recognized by anybody or anything to continue doing what I'm doing now. Why would I want to put myself under someone's control?"[33]

MC Amin's sentiment was not shared by a large number of rappers. Most of them said they would join the syndicate if they created a "rapper" or "hip-hop artist" category. But why would these rappers want to become a part of the "system" that they seem to oppose so vigorously? Why do the artists measure the legitimacy of their artistic expression based on the *naqaba*'s recognition? The answers to these questions are quite complicated, and this became evident in the rappers' responses. It was hard for them to articulate a desire for recognition from the syndicate. Regardless of whether the rappers oppose the system and all the various governmental and power structures that exist within Egypt, they still have to function within it, like any other Egyptian citizen. These artists still carry their state-issued national identification cards and most are also passport holders. They work day jobs and pay taxes like everyone else. So while they oppose the system as a whole, they still recognize that the system affords them rights. Their national identification cards and passports allow them to travel in and outside of Egypt to perform. The syndicate card would also allow them certain rights, and the right to perform is critical on multiple levels. Many hip-hop artists consider their music to be an essential part of their being. However, as the syndicate refuses to add a category for the rappers, they continue to reject the offer to be a member under the title of monologist.

By refusing to accept this categorization, Egyptian rappers are

---

33 Conversation with MC Amin, April 2013.

attempting to open up new cultural possibilities. Rather than simply playing by the rules, they seek to incite change despite the consequences. They are actively imagining a less restrictive and more nuanced cultural landscape in Egypt.

"I'm Not Selling Shit for Anybody": Oppositional Hip-Hop and the Market

As evidenced throughout this chapter, Egyptian hip-hop artists are constantly positioning themselves as "artists for a cause." By shaping their music around varying degrees of opposition, they continuously reinforce the central role the message plays in their music. At the same time, these artists do not deny that they would like to be famous. Of course, the responses for why they want to be famous differ greatly. Some assert that fame will lead to a wider audience, which will lead to more people consuming and supporting their socially and politically conscious messages. Others say that it is for the love of the hip-hop movement; they link their personal fame to the Egyptian community's overall acceptance of the genre.

In fact, some rappers are so committed to "introducing" rap into Egyptian mainstream culture that they put their "messages" to the side and participate in advertisement campaigns. Could it be that the financial gain the market has to offer proves to be just too tempting for some rappers to refuse? Is personal fame and recognition what they seek? How could the same people who speak against hegemonic powers and social injustice rap empty lyrics written for them by a major corporation to help them sell their product? Why would rappers, who produce such politically and socially charged lyrics, rap about spreadable cheese in a commercial?

It is crucial to deconstruct the notion that rap is necessarily oppositional. It is useful to consider that it is possible that some rappers "sell what sells," and it seems that, especially during times when the majority of people feel a certain degree of discontent with the political situation in their country, "opposition" certainly sells well. "Opposition" itself is a marketable commodity. Large corporations also recognize this fact. Egyptian hip-hop has recently gained attention and major companies have approached some artists to use their voices and faces to brand their products. These companies have recognized the selling potential of the artists' revolutionary messages and are hoping to cash in on the commodification of their ideas.

When I asked Egyptian hip-hop artists about advertisement campaigns, I received an array of responses. Some strongly asserted that they would not "sell shit for anybody"[34] or help any major corporations sell their products. Most of them were not so strongly opposed to the idea, as long they were allowed to write their own lyrics. Rapper E-Money explained that he was not completely against the idea of advertising a product. He said he would consider it under the conditions that he could write his own lyrics and that it was a product that he liked or believed in. I naturally asked him for examples of the types of products he would consider doing an advertisement for. Nutella was his answer.[35] Perhaps his taste for chocolate-hazelnut spread trumped his stated commitment to politically and socially conscious words, or it may be that he simply wants to make a living.

A few rappers have already participated in several advertisement campaigns. These include Snickers, Sprite, Coca-Cola, Chipsy Max (potato chips), Lion (potato chips), Tatis (another brand of potato chips), Teama Milk (spreadable cheese), and Mobinil (a major cellular service provider). A few of these advertisement campaigns were prior to the revolution but the majority were post-revolution opportunities.

The example I would like to highlight here is the Mobinil campaign. Mobinil is one of the largest cellular service providers in Egypt. It is connected to the Sawiris family, who own the Orascom Group, a conglomerate of major corporations that control much of the construction, telecommunication, and tourist services in Egypt. In the summer of 2012, when the underground scene was starting to come to the surface, Mobinil recognized an opportunity to cash in on the "resistant" artists. They approached Asfalt to participate in a collaborative song with musicians from all around Egypt called "Always Together."[36] The pay was good, and after seven years in the underground scene, this was an opportunity to air their first music video on television and their first song on the radio. They rapped a short verse that Mobinil provided for them and they shot the music video in Alexandria, where

---

34 Interview with Sphinx from Arabian Knightz, March 2013.
35 Interview with E-Money from Arabian Knightz, April 2013.
36 This song was directed by Ahmad 'Abdalla.

they performed their verses on the tram. Following the completion of recording, Mobinil asked Asfalt to sign a contract which would obligate them to six performances and limit their other appearances. This is the story of how an underground group used "opposition" to enter the mainstream and how a major corporation used an "oppositional" underground group to market their cellular service.

Conclusion

Content analysis of the music in the underground hip-hop scene points to multifaceted forms of opposition. These songs represent the artists' disapproval of hegemonic cultural, social, and political structures. Egyptian rappers often express dual forms of opposition in which they simultaneously attribute blame to both "ordinary" people and those who hold power. Some songs announce the call for change and the imagining of alternative realities. Other songs reflect the reinforcement of dominant stereotypes, attitudes, and ideologies. It is also evident that the relationship between rap and opposition is one that we must further explore, question, and deconstruct. Furthermore, the commodification of hip-hop in Egypt has already started, and it is necessary to attempt to gain a better understanding of this process and what it might mean for cultural workers who engage in this form of expression.

CHAPTER 4

Artistic Practices and Aesthetic Aims

"Everybody put your hands up!" scream the two rappers as they hop up and down on stage in unison dressed in complementary outfits complete with bow ties, suspenders, brightly colored pants, checkered shirts, and thick rimmed glasses; they grasp the attention of the entire audience. Between their perfectly articulated verses, a pop singer joins them to sing the chorus of their politically charged song; his smooth voice offers the audience a familiar sound that they can sing along with. The performers move around stage with precise motions, rotating and switching positions with ease. Every move is calculated—at one point they attempt a choreographed dance. The show is interactive—they call members of the audience to come up and help them with the chorus of their song "Who's the Target?" and they even point to me—possibly the only American in the audience of a few hundred—and laugh when they rap the lines "Shame on you, Arabs, to give in to humiliation and let your lives be ruled by the Americans!" Even such a serious statement becomes a joke during the performance. A beat-boxer joins them on stage and humorously offers a spectrum of sounds one might hear while flipping through the channels of Egyptian television. Two breakdancers join him while the rappers dance on the sidelines. This show is about entertaining an audience, not simply delivering a message.

Understanding Egyptian rap requires more than an examination of the messages of its lyrics. Focusing purely on the social and political aims of the rappers' music will lead to a shallow understanding of the artists and their practices. This chapter focuses on Egyptian rappers' embodiment of aesthetics. I will examine their tastes and how they position themselves within the underground hip-hop scene based on their ideas about 'good art.' I do not explore philosophical debates on aesthetics or attempt to present a case for why we should consider rap to be an aesthetically respectable art form. Other scholars have already considered these debates and offered valuable insight on rap as aesthetically legitimate art. For example, in his article "The Fine Art of Rap," Richard Shusterman argues that characteristics of rap such as the incorporation of new forms of technology and "an emphasis on the localized and the temporal" exemplify the postmodern aesthetic (1991:614). Popular cultural products, he points out, require new understandings and alternative imaginings of aesthetics. Mtume ya Salaam argues that 'good' art possesses attributes such as "sincerity, originality, honesty, or creativity," and is "usually emotionally involving and/or thought-provoking"—qualities he believes we find in 'good' rap (Salaam 1995:303). My interlocutors would agree that these attributes are of great importance in their music. My argument here does not seek to make a claim for the aesthetic value of hip-hop; I move forward with the understanding that it does—at least for some people—possess this value.

My interest in the aesthetics of the underground hip-hop scene in Egypt lies in the rappers' ideas of what makes good rap and enjoyable performances. In this case, art is not a transparent reflection of the relationship between class and taste, as these artists come from a diverse range of educational backgrounds, classes, and socioeconomic statuses. Pierre Bourdieu's concept of cultural capital explains the relationship among social status, "cultural knowledge," taste, upbringing, and education. One can acquire cultural capital through association with "respected" educational and other institutions, by possessing cultural goods that evidence high education or good taste (literature, art, instruments), or through the embodiment of a lifestyle associated with valuable cultural assets (this often involves growing up in an atmosphere in which others possess high amounts of cultural capital) (Bourdieu 1986:243). This concept posits that taste and social class are inextricably bound to one another and that the former is a marker of the latter. For Bourdieu, education and upbringing are critical factors in one's disposition toward the fine or popular arts (Lizardo and Skiles 2008:490). In terms of artistic consumption, Bourdieu argues that "cultural capital consists of a generalized 'aesthetic disposition'" (Lizardo and Skiles

2008:488). Bourdieu's concept works beautifully in the study of fine arts but seems to falter in the study of the popular arts, specifically in its emphasis on class.

The sociologist Sarah Thornton has built on and deviated from Bourdieu's concept of cultural capital. She proposes a "subcultural capital," which, she explains, "confers status on its owner in the eyes of the relevant beholder" (Thornton 2006:100). Thornton's subcultural capital is not as rooted in class distinctions. She primarily uses this concept to explain a type of capital which one can gain from "hipness" and being up to date with a particular scene (Thornton 2006:100). Subcultural capital can be objectified through style and dress and embodied "in the form of 'being in the know'" (Thornton 2006:100). Subcultural capital still implies that there is a hierarchy of values and taste; however, this hierarchy is not only or primarily linked to class as it is in Bourdieu's cultural capital. It is linked to the knowledge one gains outside of the social realms of particular classes and institutions; it is more often associated with the knowledge one has accumulated of a specific "art scene." Moreover, subcultural capital is linked to values such as authenticity and artistic autonomy—being outside of the dominant cultural trends (Maguadda 2009:300). The underground hip-hop community in Egypt shares some important features with subcultures: both the rappers and their followers seek to differentiate themselves from dominant, mainstream forms of popular culture. The scene also displays its subcultural qualities through fashion and musical knowledge.

Throughout this chapter, I will return to the concept of subcultural capital in order to explain some of the aesthetic practices of the artists. While I only briefly touch on audience perception and focus mostly on the community of rappers, I recognize that the role of the consumers is important and deserves more attention. It is also important to note that the rappers themselves are simultaneously consumers of this genre; they engage with the work of other artists in the scene. At concerts, there are always several established underground rappers in the audience and many aspiring rappers. I argue that the artists' aesthetics aims are focused on acts of distinction, in which they attempt to distinguish themselves from others based on their knowledge, style, and skills. These rappers have arrived at similar definitions of 'quality rap' through different introductions to the cultural field of hip-hop, but they also diverge in their emphasis on the value of specific qualities. I locate and detail three major trends of emphasis. Some rappers emphasize the importance of the poetics of rap, others focus on creating an entertaining experience, and others are concerned with delivery skills and flow. These trends point to the rappers' tastes and preferences, but also to how they use their aesthetic visions to position themselves as 'authentic' participants in the underground hip-hop scene.

Aesthetic Aims

The field of aesthetics is not its own entity that exists outside the social and political.[1] It would be worthwhile to delve further into how aesthetic and political considerations constitute one another and how the divisions between each are also sites of formation. For the purposes of this analysis, I focus on artistic understandings of aesthetic aims. Here, the term 'aesthetic aims' refers to artistic concerns with the aesthetics of the products they create and their conceptions of 'good art.' Interestingly, the artists themselves seem to separate these choices and conceptions from the content of their messages. For them, aesthetic aims are ultimately about pleasure and creating something beautiful, consumable, or entertaining. These aims seek the attention, approval, and fondness of an audience. What can we learn about the rappers' artistic practices through the lens of their aesthetic aims and the apparent separation of these aims from the political aims of their music?

While the artists I discuss here separate the 'aesthetic' from the 'political,' these divisions of form and content are not so clear. Whether it is the desire to make political statements, or the hope of recognition and fame, attention to aesthetics prevails. Just as no one wants to consume a product that comes in a messy package, potential 'consumers' are not likely to listen to a hip-hop artist's message if it is not aurally or visually pleasing. How do the artists package their messages in a way to appeal to consumers? Do all rappers in the underground hip-hop community in Egypt seek the approval of the same audience, or do their

---

1   Of course I understand that the artists acquire their artistic values and aesthetic preferences in a much larger social context and that there is a complex relationship among promoters, producers, and consumers in the artistic world; however, that discussion is beyond the scope of my exploration at this time. I hope to draw attention to these rappers' practices through a different lens.

perceptions of what is 'good art' lead them to target specific audiences? Finally, the artists must package their music in ways that appropriately and effectively convey their messages. The perceived severity of a message could be greater or lesser based on the artist's delivery. In what way do the messages themselves shape artistic choices?

This chapter will explore the artistic practices of the rappers through the lens of aesthetic aims in three ways. First, I will examine how they diverge in their conceptions of what is 'good art.' Next, I will look at how they attempt to reach and appeal to an audience. Finally, I will draw attention to the relationship between content and delivery and how these two aspects shape each other. Ted Swedenburg's comments in his article "Palestinian Rap: Against the Struggle Paradigm" speak to these questions: "[Palestinian rappers] desire to be appreciated *as artists*, and in particular, as *rap artists* who participate in a global cultural movement. In order to convey their messages effectively, moreover, it is incumbent upon them to do so in a way that is aesthetically pleasing and sensible to their listeners" (2013:18). Swedenburg draws attention to both form and content, to the political and the aesthetic. In doing so he challenges these divisions.

Exploring these questions will reveal artistic concerns of the rappers, ways in which they embody their aesthetic principles, and how certain portrayals of aesthetic preferences lead to the accumulation of subcultural capital.

The Art of Hip-Hop

Egyptian rappers in the underground scene generally say they rap because they have a message they want to convey to the world; they have something to say that they think people should hear. This is the number one reason every rapper in the hip-hop community I studied gave for why they take part in this art form. By participating in hip-hop to deliver social and political messages, these rappers hope to reinforce the power of hip-hop as an oppositional cultural product. They actively and continuously reformulate their social and cultural positions as they relate to their perception of their roles as hip-hop artists; this often leads to de-emphasizing their concerns with the aesthetic qualities of their work. This de-emphasis does not mean they are not concerned with aesthetics; rather, it reflects the performance of a role.[2] However, their narratives of how they first became interested in the genre reveal another facet of this story that deserves attention. Almost every rapper says that his initial interest in rap stemmed from liking the way it sounded when they heard other Arab or Western rappers spitting out words. They found breakdancing fascinating. They liked the beats. Initially, their attraction to rap had little to do with the messages; they focused much more on their perceived value of the art form itself.

Although Egyptian rappers participate in this art form because of their aesthetic attraction to it, they diverge in their ideas of what makes good rap. There is no consensus of what they consider to be good. Through analysis of their music, concerts, fashion, music videos, and personal reflections concerning artistic expression, I locate their differences in taste.

The "Poets," the "Entertainers," and the "Rappers for the Sake of Rap." For the purpose of this exploration of artistic practices and aesthetics in the underground hip-hop scene in Egypt, I categorize the rappers into three groups that reflect their primary artistic concerns. The first group I refer to as the "Poets"; these rappers focus on the production of meaningful poetry. They pay great attention to word choice and arrangement. They carefully choose thoughtful and eloquent language. They are concerned with rhyme, measure, meter, and the weight of words. The Poets believe that the beauty of rap lies in the delivery that can highlight their poetic verses. These rappers usually appear "as themselves" in that they perform in their everyday attire. The second group is the "Entertainers." They are concerned with creating engaging performances and entertaining music videos with storylines. They have stylists and they choreograph their shows. They seek a broader audience and incorporate artists from other genres into their songs and performances. They tend to dress in clothing that stands out and

---

2   There is a more in-depth discussion of this in chapter five. I mention this here because I have to recognize that I conducted my fieldwork in a very specific social and political climate in Egypt (I started a year after the revolution). During this time it seems (some) rappers have reformulated their roles in society as social and political critics. Emphasizing this role seems to takes precedence over everything else. During initial conversations with these rappers, they always emphasize this aspect of their art rather than discussing their aesthetic attraction to it; we could say they choose to present themselves as caring more about function than form.

goes against the dominant trends. The third group is the "Rappers for the Sake of Rap." These rappers emphasize the way they deliver their lines. They are concerned with the style of this artistic medium. They mostly comment on flow and their perceptions of one's ability to rap. Most of the rappers in this group call their music and their delivery "hard core." These rappers generally adopt the style people tend to associate with Western hip-hop—oversized t-shirts, baggy pants, and sometimes baseball caps. Of course there is overlap in these categories; my aim here is simply to draw attention to the trends in the scene. All of them are indeed concerned with the entertainment aspect of their work; however, each type of artist highlights a specific aspect of the art form as constituting 'good rap.' I can identify at least four artists who fit into each of these groups.[3]

All three groups embody their aesthetic concerns and produce images of themselves that represent these concerns. For example, Zap Tharwat, one of the Poets, often posts pictures on Facebook and other social media that evoke a calm scene in which he is the thoughtful intellectual. In figure 4, he sits holding a book (of his own poetry) and allows the viewer a glimpse into his artistic practice. Could he be thinking of his next great idea for one of his lyrical masterpieces? Is he reflecting on a poem he has already written? When Zap speaks about other rappers in the underground scene, it is obvious that his preferences lean toward some of the other Poets. When he comments on the work of other rappers, he generally frames his critique around the quality of the word, the cleverness of the rhymes, and the arrangement of the song. We listened to the music of another Poet, Deeb; Zap was immediately attracted to a simple acoustic track with powerful lyrics and a tight arrangement. Zap appreciates the work of rappers whose aesthetic concerns are in line with his own. Among the other rappers, Zap is known for his writing. When other rappers commented on him, no one denied that he is a good *writer*; however, some of the Entertainers and the Rappers

---

3   After I decided to categorize the rappers using these three groups, I decided to test my idea by asking the rappers where they locate themselves and other rappers according to my divisions. Interestingly, I found that nearly every time, rappers would place themselves and their peers in the same categories I chose for them. This shows how the rappers themselves identify clear divisions within the scene.

Fig. 4. Zap Tharwat

for the Sake of Rap criticized him as a *rapper*. One[4] commented, "Yes, Zap writes very well. His *words* are powerful. But that doesn't mean he should call himself a rapper. He is not a rapper." This rapper's opinion constitutes an act of distinction. He is a rapper but Zap is not, because they do not share the same aesthetic concerns or definitions of 'good rap.' In this sense, his critique is the assertion of his subcultural capital. He hopes to bring attention to the "fact" that he *knows* what real rap is while Zap does not. According to this rapper and others similar to him, they are participating in authentic rap while Zap is not. However, Zap's fans (and fellow Poets) would disagree. There are at least three Facebook pages (aside from his own artist page) that are dedicated to praising Zap Tharwat as the "best rapper in Egypt."[5] Fans emphasize Zap's "real" qualities—he does not dress in "costumes," he does not copy any other rappers, he simply expresses what is in his heart.[6] These types

---

4 This rapper asked that I keep his name anonymous if I wrote about his comments on other rappers. I place him with the Rappers for the Sake of Rap.

5 See, for example, the Zap Tharwat "Ultras" page: https://www.facebook.com/UltrasZapTharwat

6 Various comments posted by fans.

of comments suggest an association with some "pure" unmediated art form. This is also a quality of subcultural capital; the fans perceive Zap as an 'autonomous' rapper who does not conform to mainstream cultural trends or the artistic trends of the scene. Fans who have deep knowledge of the scene reassert Zap's subcultural capital by identifying him as unique and "real."

The rap duo Asfalt, Ibrahim Farouk and Gad Kareem, are the performers I described at the opening of this chapter. They are the best representation of the Entertainers, and it seems that other hip-hop acts with the same sense of what makes good rap have started to follow their lead. Performance quality is a primary concern. They seek to make their fans laugh, dance, and have an all-around 'hip-hop experience' complete with singers, breakdancers, and beat-boxers. The photograph in figure 5, like the picture of Zap (fig. 4), captures the artists' embodied aesthetic concerns. They actively produce an image that evokes a sense of energy and humor. Their attention to their image is apparent in their carefully planned, quirky outfits and the retro-style background, which exemplify

Fig. 5. Asfalt (Ibrahim Farouk and Gad Kareem)

their concern with the visual aspect of their art. Most rappers in the underground scene generally praise Ibrahim and Gad for their attention to performance. The image of the performer and entertainer is one that Ibrahim maintains in his daily life. He has embodied the entertainer; when fans stop him at outdoor cafés he never disappoints. One might find him fiddling with his clunky silver rings, wearing coral pants and a stylish scarf. In the Egyptian rap scene, the members of Asfalt win in terms of originality. While some rappers (particularly among the Rappers for the Sake of Rap) comment on their skills as rappers or their tendency to lean toward a more mainstream "pop" sound, no one disputes that they consistently put on entertaining performances. As F Killa told me, "Asfalt is the only group that puts on a real show and understands performance."[7] Asfalt's music is upbeat, their songs are generally easy to follow, and their choruses are catchy. Additionally, they carefully plan their performances down to the last details of body positioning, gestures, and jokes.

Returning to the concept of subcultural capital, Asfalt's audience presents an interesting site of examination. They use various techniques to assert their knowledge of the scene and attempt to prove they are "in the know." Attendees of Asfalt's concerts use the space as an opportunity to engage in the display of their subcultural capital. Some fans "spontaneously" breakdance below the stage. This is an opportunity to show one's status of having an intimate connection with the hip-hop scene. It is an assertion of familiarity with the genre and a performance of their hipness. It is not only about showing one's skills, but is also an affirmation of membership. Moreover, the successful execution of a spontaneous performance allows the amateur breakdancers to look as if they are not trying too hard, but rather that they embody a particular lifestyle.[8] Another way for audience members to gain subcultural capital is to sing or rap along with the lyrics. These concert-goers show their knowledge of the music. This works especially well when the performers are rapping a relatively new song and only a few audience members are rapping along. However, this is also a point in which one can lose sub-

---

7   Interview with F Killa, April 2013. I classify F Killa with the Rappers for the Sake of Rap.
8   After much observation, I suspect that the amateur breakdancers probably rehearse and plan the "spontaneous" performances.

The Art of Hip-Hop

cultural capital by appearing too eager or too enthusiastic, such as the fans who try to make sure their voice is heard over others. The successful accumulation of subcultural capital rests on one's ability to demonstrate knowledge with ease; they must prove that they know what is happening and that they are engaged, but not overly excited.

Arabian Knightz are Rappers for the Sake of Rap. They exemplify the embodiment of the 'rapper attitude.' They are serious, but they express this seriousness in a very different manner from the Poets. While this seriousness comes through in their performances, videos, and songs (lyrics and music), they also carry it through in every image I have ever seen. Just as in figure 6, they do not ever smile when they pose. They must keep consistent with their image of being dedicated "knightz" fighting for the Arab cause. They exude a vibe that tells us they are not taking their job lightly. They send the message that their work is meaningful and important and urge potential consumers to consider it as such. But their self-portayal is not purely about their "cause" (which has more to do with the content of their music); it is also about their commitment to the craft of rap.

During an interview with E-Money, he spent almost two hours discussing what makes good hip-hop and which rappers in Egypt are good or not. He told me the story of how he came to be E-Money of

Fig. 6. Arabian Knightz (E-Money, Rush, and Sphinx)

Arabian Knightz. He was member of the group Asfalt in 2005 and left the group due to artistic differences. This departure signifies a difference in aesthetic values of the rappers. E-Money was freestyling at a club one night when he met Sphinx. When Sphinx heard E-Money's flow, he was impressed and told him, "Your flow is money!" E-Money's given name is Ehab, and this is how they arrived at "E-Money." During our discussion he repeatedly referred to his "fast flow" as one of the reasons he believes he is a good rapper. He told me, "I get aggressive on the mic." He complained about other rappers in the underground hip-hop scene in Egypt and said that "they dumb down the flow so that people can get it." He explained:

> *Rap is rhythm and poetry; rhythm is first and poetry is second. If we were supposed to focus more on poetry it woud be called "par." After hearing most of the rappers here you are not going to leave feeling amazed by the flow, you are going to leave saying, "Nice words." I mean you have to flow with the beat. If this country becomes okay and everything's nice and fine, what is your rap going to be worth?*[9]

For E-Money the aesthetic value of rap lies completely in the delivery. For him, rap is a talent that exists independent of one's ability to write good lyrics or to put on a show. Moreover, E-Money's emphasis on his knowledge of rap is a way to position himself in the scene. His assertions attack the authenticity of rappers who do not emphasize rhythm over poetry or flow over words. He went on to rap a verse in a song titled "Wack MCz," which critiques rappers for their poor rap skills. He and the other two rappers in the song distinguish themselves as the opposite of the bad rappers they describe. Among the Rappers for the Sake of Rap and their followers, E-Money possesses a high amount of subcultural capital. His capital comes in both embodied and objectified forms and reflects his aesthetic preferences. His dress typically consists of a large t-shirt with something written on it such as "Arab Hip-Hop" or "Arabs Stand Up," jean shorts or pants, a gold rope chain, and some sort of hat (fig. 7). In one sense, his style reflects his knowledge of the broader global hip-hop scene. But in another way, he subtly rejects claims of imitation. For example, when I asked him about his

---

9   Interview with E-Money, March 2013.

Packaging

Fig. 7. E-Money

style, he told me he wears what he thinks is comfortable; a big t-shirt and jeans is a relaxed way to dress—he is not so concerned with appearance and this is certainly a way to reinforce his hipness. The gold rope chain, he explains, was a gift, so he is not being "showy" or attempting to "look like a rapper," but exhibiting the proper courtesy of showing appreciation for a gift.[10] As Thorton asserts, "Nothing depletes capital more than the sight of someone trying too hard" (2006:101). Therefore, even if he is "trying," he explains his choices logically to make it seem as if he is not.

Packaging

In his study of Palestinian rap, Swedenburg asserts that "for Palestinian hip-hop to be politically effective, it cannot *only* be about the 'message,'" and that "in order to win over audiences, both local and foreign, Palestinian rappers must necessarily be concerned with aesthetics, with

---
10 Interview with E-Money, March 2013.

production of 'good art'" (2013:18). This necessity of the 'art' in relation to the 'message' was never more apparent than when I attended a concert for the Egyptian Hip-Hop Union in which around eight hip-hop acts performed. I arrived in the middle of a set of an artist who was rapping about the same topics all the other rappers are rapping about during the current period of social and political change and stasis—revolution, politics, and social concerns—but the audience was not responding. It simply did not sound good. His music and delivery were not pleasing to the ear, nor was his performance pleasing to the eye. It was boring. He became frustrated and gave one last attempt to draw in the audience by commenting on their lack of enthusiasm in a jumbled mix of English and Arabic phrases, "Make some noooooooooise! Come on guys, are you sleeping (*yalla ya shabab, intu naymin*)? Are you tired (*ta'banin*)? Wake up and make some noise! Let me hear you! Forget it, I'm tired (*khalas ana ta'ibt*)." The unresponsive audience's silence finally pushed him to graciously thank them for attending and then leave the stage. Following this act, another group burst onto the stage full of energy and "better quality"[11] music and the audience woke up.

I recount this experience to emphasize the notion that in order for the rappers' music to be effective, they have to appeal to an audience. This requires both 'good' music and an idea of the audience's expectations. The ways in which the artists package their music reflect their preferences as well as their knowledge of the scene or their subcultural capital. The rapper who failed in his performance did not have the same conception of 'good art' as the audience that rejected him. The other acts in the Egyptian Hip-Hop Union show consisted mostly of the Entertainers I described earlier. This rapper was out of place. The Entertainers produce "fun" music (generally regardless of the message), and if they do perform a serious song, they are able to make it a pleasurable experience by incorporating intense movement and seemingly contagious energy. I believe this rapper did not possess the subcultural capital he needed to engage the audience. In addition to the 'bad' music and 'poor' performance, he seemed to be trying to be an 'authentic' rapper but did

---

11 I do not refer to my own opinion of the value of the music. The 'quality' of music in the underground rap scene ranges; some pay professional producers for arrangements, some allow their amateur producer friends to arrange beats, and others download tracks from the Internet.

not have the appropriate knowledge of the scene. Moreover, in his last attempt, in which he shouted out phrases in English, some audience members reacted with laughter as if to express their disapproval of his seemingly forced attempt to be 'cool.'

On the other hand, the use of English can be well received if done in a way that people perceive as authentic. The rapper who failed to impress the audience with his code-switching also failed to convince them that English was a natural part of his everyday speech. In this way, they perceived his code-switching as a sad attempt to pretentiously show off his status or assert that he was from a particular class of people who speak English and Arabic interchangeably.

Another rapper, Sphinx from Arabian Knightz, almost always raps in English, but the other two members generally rap in Arabic. Sphinx grew up in the US and moved to Egypt in 2005 after graduating from college in California. When I asked other rappers what they thought about Sphinx rapping in English, they generally approved because they believed that he "feels" this language—it is not an attempt to be cool, but rather an authentic expression of his thoughts and feelings. Additionally, by "packaging" some of their messages in English, Arabian Knightz are able to appeal to a broader listening audience. While Sphinx's English is stronger than his Arabic (which seems reason enough to choose to rap in English), Arabian Knightz redefines their use of English and suggests that it is a method to deconstruct stereotypes of Arabs, speak directly to oppressive powers, and inform the English-speaking audience of the concerns of Arabs.[12] Thus, Sphinx has the capability and the credibility to 'represent' to an English-speaking audience. This explanation allows the members of Arabian Knightz to reassert their authenticity even while engaging in a practice that rappers in the scene would generally criticize and reject.

In addition to packaging music to make it enjoyable so that people are more likely to listen to what they have to say, most rappers in the scene also share the goal of reaching a wider audience and introducing hip-hop to a broader Egyptian listening public. They go about this in a variety of ways, such as collaborating with underground soft rock bands and alternative pop singers. In this way they can attract listeners who may be fans of the Egyptian underground music scene, but not neces-

---

12 Interview with Sphinx, March 2013.

sarily of hip-hop. This technique is employed more by the Poets and the Entertainers, and less by the Rappers for the Sake of Rap, who generally rap their own choruses rather than opting for a singer.

One of the rappers in the Rappers for the Sake of Rap group, MC Amin, asserts through social media that he does hard-core rap. Amin's music appears to display no interest in reaching a broader audience. He uses rough, harsh language and often curses. He seems to rap for other rappers. The Poets and the Entertainers have diverse fan bases, and a good percentage of their concert attendees are teenage girls wearing headscarves. MC Amin is obviously not targeting this audience. However, he recently started packaging his songs in a way that is distinct from all the other rappers in the scene. Amin chose to collaborate with *mahraganat* musicians.[13] *Mahraganat* is one of the newest and most popular forms of music in Egypt. Its innovators come from some of the poorest neighborhoods in Cairo, where the genre first spread after its introduction at local street weddings and celebrations. Its combination of highly auto-tuned and sometimes offensive lyrics, electronic music, recycled beats, and local popular (*sha'bi*) dance rhythms make *mahraganat* a uniquely appealing genre.[14] As of now, the *mahraganat* consumers in Egypt outnumber the hip-hop consumers by far.[15] MC Amin stated that he wanted to participate in the collaboration for the possibility of introducing listeners to hip-hop and its messages. He explained that his actions were not an attempt to *appeal*, but rather to *introduce* and give people the opportunity to become familiar with the genre. He said that even if only 20 percent of the *mahraganat* listeners became hip-hop fans, he would be satisfied. MC Amin asserted that he was not incorporating this type of music to become more famous or

---

13 *Mahraganat* translates as 'festivals'; however, it is the also the name of a new genre of music in Egypt. Interestingly, some of the *mahraganat* artists label themselves as rappers. This generally does not please rappers, who regard the two music forms as separate.

14 Some of the popular *mahraganat* artists have performed internationally. Even within Egypt, these artists perform across social classes—they perform at local street weddings as well as extravagant hotel weddings. Their appeal is widespread and seems to have no class boundaries.

15 The hip-hop act with the most Facebook likes is at about 140,000 (which is rare in the hip-hop scene), while the popular *mahragan* acts such as Oka and Ortega, Sadat, and Fifty have close to one million likes on their artist pages.

Packaging

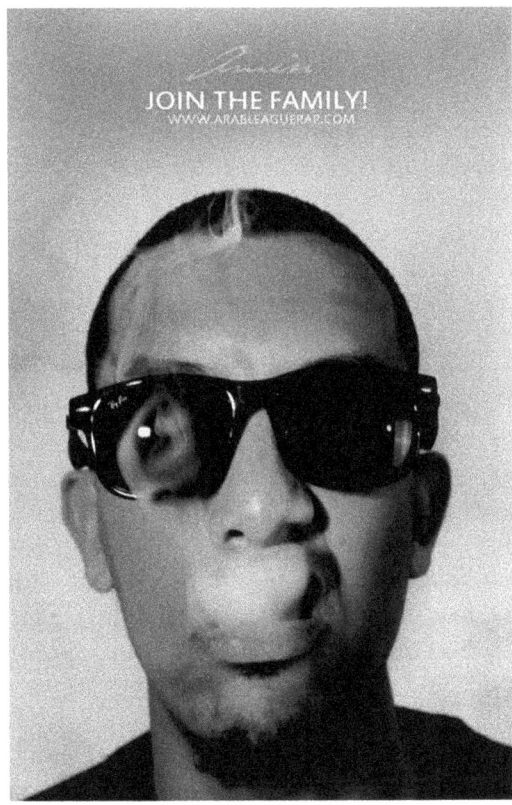

Fig. 8. MC Amin

"ride the wave" of a new, popular trend.[16] However, as MC Amin's reputation among the rap community and his fans is that of a "real" hard-core rapper,[17] they did not unanimously support his decision to move away from the more "pure" form of rap that he previously produced. Former fans posted critical comments to express their disappointment. In the eyes of the hip-hop listening community, MC Amin's departure from 'authentic' rap depleted some of his subcultural capital; they viewed his actions as selling out to gain popularity.

These examples show some of the ways in which artists package their messages to provide an aesthetic experience for consumers, which leads

---

16 Interview with MC Amin, March 2013.
17 He is from the city of Mansura, which actually seems to give him street credibility among rappers from Cairo.

to the consumption of the artists' social and political messages. Here, it is important to recognize that rappers use nuanced packaging techniques to appeal to different audiences, both local and foreign. However, these methods of packaging, which are not always in line with the artists' self-portrayal and earlier aesthetic aims, sometimes lead members of the hip-hop scene to question the artists' originality. Regardless, it is evident that the rappers are certainly concerned with the aesthetic value of their music, and they realize that effectively reaching an audience depends largely on the creation of a pleasurable experience or an enjoyable product.

How the Message Shapes the Delivery

In order for Egyptian rappers to convey their messages in an effective manner, the delivery must appropriately reflect the tone of the message. Effective delivery is about producing a believable product. Rapping about politics and social concerns requires a certain degree of seriousness. It is clear that there is a relationship between the lyrical content of the rappers' music and the delivery of this content. The rappers desire to put on a believable performance in which people can feel and experience the severity, importance, and necessity of their words.

Aly Talibab, one of the Poets, shouts each line of his songs. He stands in the middle of a stage but he cannot keep his body still. He holds onto the microphone stand and thrusts his body with every word he screams. He is powerful. It is impossible not to look at or listen to Aly when he performs. He often performs in public spaces such as high-traffic areas in downtown Cairo. The power of his delivery catches the attention of ordinary passersby. In Aly's case, content and delivery style intersect. Aly Talibab only raps about serious issues and often incorporates his deep, conflicting, philosophical concerns into his music. He seems to feel that, in order for anyone to take his messages as seriously as he does, he must convey them in a very particular manner. This also leads to the question of the choice of medium. Rap is about the shouting out of words, and for Aly Talibab it is the most powerful and effective genre to express his messages.

While Talibab uses his body and the volume of his voice to demand critical consideration of content, other artists use their music videos to visually express their messages. Some rappers find their messages to be

How the Message Shapes the Delivery

Fig. 9. Aly Talibab

of such importance that, rather than incorporating a story or plot in their music videos, they simply flash the lyrics across the screen. The rappers explained that this choice stems from their concern that, because of rap's rapid and complicated delivery, they find it necessary to visually enforce their messages. Sphinx explained that "I have something important to say, and if they are not going to understand it when I spit it, they are going to understand it when they read it."[18]

Other rappers do produce videos with plots. An interesting example is the collaboration between Zap Tharwat and Asfalt in their 2011 song "Writing a Letter for Tomorrow." The members of Asfalt put their generally quirky style and light vibe to the side, as this message required a serious tone. The video opens with an image of Zap lying on the dirt floor of an abandoned building; he is tied at his ankles and mouth. He slowly sits up and struggles to tear the cloth tied over his mouth. During the fourth line of the song he says, "I exist and I don't exist, living without a voice," and a few lines later he continues, "because words in

---

18 Interview with Sphinx, March 2013.

our country never reach." Thus the video reinforces the words and takes them to a new symbolic level. In the video he is in a place where no one would ever hear him; he is completely alone in a deserted building. If no one can hear him, does he exist? What is the point of existing if your words do not carry meaning or effect change? In this case, through visual performance Zap takes his statements to a deeper level and allows viewers to further interpret his message.

Conclusion

Throughout the course of my fieldwork, it became apparent that the aesthetic choices, tastes, and preferences in the hip-hop scene in Egypt and the Arab world deserve much more attention. Specifically in times of social and political upheaval, journalists, filmmakers, and scholars tend to focus solely on the messages found in the lyrics of this art form. I have found that the messages are of extreme importance to the artists themselves, and rappers tend to define themselves by the messages in their music. However, most of them started because of their interest in the aesthetic qualities of the art form itself, not because of an interest in using this medium as some form of resistance. Egyptian rappers differ in their conceptions of 'good art,' and more specifically in their definitions of 'good rap.' They embody these conceptions through their practices. While they diverge in their aesthetic values, it is also crucial that if they want people to consume their messages, they must package them in an appealing manner. Packaging targets specific audiences. Moreover, it is also evident that sometimes the message itself shapes other artistic choices, as illustrated in the various ways rappers make their lyrics accessible to audiences. Finally, the aesthetic preferences and assertions of the rappers and fans are a crucial site of subcultural capital and the ways in which knowledge of the scene enhances one's status within it. Subcultural capital leads to mobility within the scene, such as when fans can use their capital to convert themselves from consumers to producers. Ultimately 'art' matters a great deal in the Egyptian underground hip-hop scene.

CHAPTER 5

Identity Formation in the Egyptian Underground Hip-Hop Scene

Egyptian underground hip-hop, a form of cultural production, is a crucial site for the examination of identity formation. Critical analyses of cultural products consider the historical, economic, political, and social factors that contribute to their formation. The same factors are crucial in examining how cultural workers form their subjectivities. Identity formation in the cultural field is a confluence of how artists feel about themselves in a particular time and space as well the expectations of the field itself. Cultural products act as a site of identity formation in two ways: the artists form their identities through their products and self-portrayal, and the products they create also act as sites for consumers to formulate and experience particular aspects of their identities. Identity can contract and expand at specific moments. For example, song lyrics have the ability to trigger something inside listeners, which could intensify their identification with one facet of their identity. While studying how music and other cultural products contribute to the identity formation of consumers is worthwhile, I focus here on the identity formation of the artists themselves. This chapter explores how Egyptian hip-hop artists in the underground scene shape their identities through their practices. Lyrics, performative self-representation, and social media are all venues to explore the rappers' constructions of their identities. By approaching identity formation as a fluid process, I will reveal how aspects of the Egyptian hip-hop artists' identities fluctuate in times of revolution, social and political change, and stasis.

In addition to understanding the process of identity formation within a broader social context, I also question how the rapper begins to *feel* he is a rapper. This examination will consider the individual practices that the rappers perform to cultivate their 'rapper selves.' Thus, this study will not only address 'outward' identity formation in terms of how the rappers perform, assert, and position themselves, it will also look at 'inward' identity formation in terms of the practices that contribute to the creation of a specific internal disposition.

Identity and Symbolic Capital

Conceptual work on identity as outlined in the field of cultural studies, in particular that of Stuart Hall, and the theoretical work of Pierre Bourdieu inform my exploration of identity formation. In engaging these theories and concepts, I explore the struggle over symbolic capital in the underground hip-hop community. I use the term 'identity,' as Hall does in much of his work, as a process rather than an essence. Hall asserts that the concept of identity is "strategic and positional" and that identities are "increasingly fragmented and fractured; never singular but multiply constructed across different, often intersecting and antagonistic, discourses, practices and positions" (1996:3–4). Identities are not static and must be considered within a social and historical context. People shape their identities in relation to what is happening around them. As this study is concerned with how artists form and *perform* their identities through music, Simon Frith's remarks on the relationship between music and identity are valuable to consider. He states, "Music, like identity, is both performance and story, describes the social in the individual and the individual in the social, the mind in the body and the body in the mind" (Frith 1996:109). Artists tell stories through their music and use these stories to position themselves within the broader social world that surrounds them.

Identity is a fluid process; it changes and is reflective of time and space. For example, what it means to be an Egyptian now, in times of revolution, carries different implications than before February 11, 2011.[1] Rappers' emphasis on being politically involved suggests a new requirement for a 'good' Egyptian in the underground scene. Identity has multiple layers, some more negotiable than others. While I do not believe in a stable core of the self, I do believe there are some aspects of our identities we are more willing to do away with, put to the side,

---

1   The day former Egyptian president Hosni Mubarak stepped down after 18 consecutive days of protesters demanding that he remove himself from power.

or even "sell" in some cases. Egyptian hip-hop artists are rarely willing to negotiate their "resistant" or "activist" self, but may be willing to sacrifice their "creative" or "original" self in pursuit of economic or symbolic capital.

Bourdieu's concept of field, in which agents struggle over control of different forms of capital, provides a framework to understand the rappers' positioning of their identities and helps us to interpret the motivation for some of their practices. I conceptualize the Egyptian underground hip-hop scene as its own field within the broader cultural field. Bourdieu posits that fields are "arenas for struggle of legitimation" (Swartz 1997:123). Egyptian hip-hop artists function within a set of rules, values, and norms of the field. These rules govern the production of hip-hop, and the members of the underground hip-hop community implicitly comply with these rules through their involvement. If the artists play by the rules of the field, producers and consumers of underground hip-hop will view them as "legitimate" hip-hop artists. The artists in the field of Egyptian hip-hop are struggling over specific resources such as reputation, honor, recognition, "authenticity," legitimacy, and prestige. These values are what Bourdieu refers to as symbolic capital. Bourdieu views the cultural world as the economic world in reverse. The values in the cultural field inherently oppose those in the economic world. Rather than fighting for economic capital, actors in the cultural field are fighting for symbolic capital; each rapper wants fans and other artists in the community to consider him a "real" artist, an activist, a revolutionary, and an intellectual. Furthermore, the values of the underground hip-hop scene dictate, to some extent, how the artists form, position, and represent their identities.

The Field of Egyptian Underground Hip-Hop

Before discussing how the Egyptian underground hip-hop scene acts as a site of identity formation, I will briefly trace the values of the field. Creativity, originality, and authenticity are important among these. Rappers frequently comment on their own and others' creativity in order to represent and distinguish themselves as "real" artists. Hip-hop artists also value skills such as 'flow' and the ability to write "clever" lyrics that hold meaning. It is equally important to deliver these creative ideas in ways that showcase the rapper's talent. Popularity and recognition are desired resources; underground hip-hop artists measure success according to who books the most concerts, who has the most "likes" on their Facebook pages, and who has the most views of their YouTube videos. Political and social awareness, morality, and spirituality are not only crucial values, but also subjects that rappers must address to be part of the scene. The artists use their "authority" on these issues to distance themselves from "ordinary" people and speak on their behalf. Involvement in the revolution and writing about revolutionary ideas are credentials by which Egyptian rappers assert their legitimacy. Hip-hop artists use the revolution as a temporal marker; they discuss what they were doing before, during, and after the revolution. The artists who have the greatest legitimacy are the rappers who were writing about political issues prior to the revolution, went to the Square during the revolution, and continue to fight against oppression after the revolution.

Moreover, agents in the field rely on social capital, the relationships which enable the acquisition of resources (such as symbolic capital), in order to accumulate and sustain legitimacy (Bourdieu 1986:252). Bourdieu points out that "individuals and groups draw upon a variety of cultural, social, and symbolic resources in order to maintain and enhance their position in the social order" (Swartz 1997:73). Social capital contributes to the strength of the artists' claims of authenticity and legitimacy. As Bourdieu views all forms of capital as sources of power, agents who accumulate a fair amount of social capital have greater ability to control what happens in the field. Artists accumulate social capital by forming alliances with other artists who similarly locate their identities and seem to share the same values. These alliances contribute to the struggle over symbolic capital and identity formation: members of these alliances often take part in the "us" and "them" discourse—we represent "this" and they represent "that."

While I choose to engage the underground hip-hop scene as its own field, I also recognize that this particular field does not have internal consistency and is indeed influenced by outside forces such as the social and political context in which it exists. Additionally, identity formation is not limited to the artist's position in the field; identities are formed in multiple frames. In this sense, it is useful to briefly depart from the concept of field and explore other venues that reveal alternative processes of the rappers' creation of their 'rapper selves.'

The Embodiment of the Rapper

Egyptian rappers are performers. Both on stage and off, they carefully craft and reassert their practices. They also performed throughout the interviews and the additional time I spent with them, presenting themselves to me as a 'rapper,' which could differ from how they act around close friends and family.[2] However, there is more to this story than two separate selves existing independently of one another. I believe these individuals have embodied their rapper selves through years of training and internalizing their values by different methods.

Many of these rappers have been involved in this scene for over five years, and some for more than 10. They all have stories of how they have "become" a rapper. These stories reveal specific practices that contribute to the formation of the 'rapper self,' such as ways of dressing, moving, and speaking. I am interested in how the rappers' external practices help to shape their rapper selves and will attempt to identify some specific practices that contribute to the inner building of the rapper.

Training. When Zap first started rapping in 2008, he did not *feel* like a rapper. When he first performed on stage, he would stand in the middle and rap his verses but he would not move. He explained to me that his lack of movement did not come from fear or the anxiety of performance, but from the fact that he felt like he was acting. He believed that good rappers feel the beat and move to the music and that there is something natural about this, and he did not have this natural feeling. Of course he recognized that movement also makes for a more entertaining performance. However, for Zap the ability to move was about feeling like a "true" rapper who would be able to spontaneously take over the stage. He wanted to become a physical representation of his music.

I came across this information one night directly following one of Zap's performances. He sat silently, with a reflective stare. When I asked

---

2 A discussion of performativity would be useful in this exploration, in that I agree that exterior practices are not reflections of some interior essence of the self and that actually exterior practices shape our conceptions of identity. However, as performativity studies are largely centered on discourse and speech acts (although Judith Butler also considers bodily performative acts as well), this discussion is beyond the scope of my exploration. Here I simply seek to highlight a few examples of how we can understand the relationship between the construction of the self and external practices. Saba Mahmood's work in *Politics of Piety* inspired my line of thinking.

him what he was thinking about, he told me that he was happy, and that he finally felt like a rapper. This statement was confusing to me since Zap had been rapping for over four years. He went on to tell me that "it just happened" and that the movements finally came "all of the sudden ... by themselves."[3] He elaborated on the transformation by explaining that he had to train himself to feel like a rapper. Over the next hour he recounted forcing himself to move his body to every beat he heard, lifting his shoulders, and nodding his head.

He revealed that he finally "naturally" moves to beats, acts out every word, and uses his body in various ways for emphasis. I have been attending Zap's concerts for over a year, and I was able to witness some of these changes. He is now confident and it is apparent to anyone who watches him perform that he feels what he is doing. I understand we could view Zap's transformation as one that he initiated through practice; however, I believe this is not just about the practice of performance. Through training and repeated movement Zap can now spontaneously produce a seemingly effortless enactment of the songs (both beats and lyrics). He trained himself to cultivate an inner feeling of "being" a rapper.

During a conversation with another rapper, E-Money, I asked him when he started to feel like a rapper. He told me he started rapping in 2003 and said that when he first started he dressed "normal." I assume this meant he dressed in a similar manner to his peers. He told me that during this time, he felt that he was a "guy who raps" rather than a rapper. He said, "I did not really feel like a rapper until after I started wearing this kind of clothes."[4] He was wearing a cap, a large t-shirt, and baggy pants. He told me this is now the only way he dresses and he would not feel like himself without this type of clothing. He started to feel he was a rapper through repeatedly dressing in this manner and now he would feel uncomfortable if he were to wear anything else. In this way, it seems that through the external practice of dress, E-Money created an inner sense of self.

While this is only a preliminary exploration of the creation of the internal feeling of the 'rapper self' through bodily practices, I think this is a valuable site for further investigation. Art and skill always require training, but these examples evidence that cultivation of the sense of the artistic self requires extensive training and repetition. I turn now to how

---

3   Conversation with Zap, October 2012.
4   Interview with E-Money, April 2012.

these rappers interact with one another in the field and the techniques they use to shape their identities.

The "I"

Hip-hop artists in the underground scene use their music and various forms of media to make self-assertions; close examination of these assertions reveals how these rappers locate their social and cultural roles. There are various forms of "Who am I?" or "This is my life" songs that many of the artists release in order to introduce themselves to the listeners. These songs tell the listeners not only who the artist *is*, but who the artist *is not*. The combination of self-assertions, which we can examine through the statements they write on their Facebook pages in addition to the biographical narratives they tell through their songs, point to the artists' formation of their subjectivities. Furthermore, the "I" points to how the artists conceptualize their collective identities; they situate themselves as members of particular groups. They position themselves as belonging to these groups through methods of self-labeling as well as by addressing issues important to other members.

Naming. Many Egyptian hip-hop artists have 'rap names.' This is pertinent not only in exploring how rappers view themselves and their practices, but also provides insight into which aspects of their identity the rappers prioritize. Why is it, for example, that some rappers use terms such as "Arab" or "Egyptian" in the process of self-labeling? Sometimes the rap name carries a specific meaning, while other times the artists chose a nickname they grew up with, or use a shortened or altered version of their given name. By taking part in naming, the artists are also positioning and locating themselves as *rappers*. Other artists in the Egyptian underground music scene do not participate in the naming process; this is specific to the hip-hop scene. One group calls themselves "Arabian Knightz;" this name, they argue, expresses the primary goals of their music: to promote Arab unity and to "fight for the Arab cause."[5] The members of Arabian Knightz use a play on words; they use the word 'knight' as in 'fighter,' while simultaneously referencing the book *One Thousand and One Nights*.[6] They assert that their aim is to tell stories

---

5   Interview with Sphinx from Arabian Knightz, March 2012.
6   *Alf layla wa layla*, which most people in the English speaking world would know as *Arabian Nights*.

through their music.⁷ Arabian Knightz also emphasize an "Arab identity" (as opposed to an "Egyptian identity") through all of their practices, including the way they dress. They often wear Palestinian *kufiya* scarves to express their dedication to Arab solidarity, and they even have their own line of t-shirts bearing messages like "Captain Arabia" or "Arabs Stand Up." Another rapper goes by two names, one in English and the other in Arabic: F Killa and al-Muqatil. He explained that F Killa refers to 'flow killer.' He said he can rap using nuanced 'flows' and that he is so talented that he 'kills' all of them.⁸ F Killa transformed the meaning of *al-muqatil* (which translates as 'fighter'), and explains that he arrived at this rap name by combining the first syllable of his given name, Muhammad (Mu), and the Arabic word for 'killer' (*qatil*).⁹ Another group calls themselves Asfalt ('asphalt'); they chose this name to express the mundane and the everyday. The two members of Asfalt assert that they rap about everyday problems and relate to "normal" people who come from the same streets they do. By choosing this name, Asfalt present themselves as "one of the people." It would be interesting to further examine how the process of self-labeling shapes the lyrical content of the artists' music. Could it be that by naming or labeling himself the artist feels the need to live up to the name in hopes of being viewed as legitimate by his audience and other artists in the scene?

The artists carefully choose their names to represent what they stand for or how they want people to perceive them. Some of these names emphasize aesthetic qualities, while others make a statement of principle. While there is a diverse set of rap names among the artists, they all tend to agree that they are part of the underground scene.¹⁰ Accepting and using the underground label implies that each of these artists is willing to comply with the rules, values, and expectations of the field. The use of this underground label means that audiences and other rappers expect these artists to address only specific topics. For example, an artist could potentially lose his legitimacy if he released a romantic song rather than a socially or politically conscious song.

---

7   Conversation with Sphinx, April 2013.
8   Interview with F Killa, April 2013.
9   Interview with F Killa, April 2013.
10 I provide a thorough explanation of how artists understand the meaning of 'underground' in chapter one.

Thus, being underground allows for a space to form their identities and artistic practices.

The Battle of the "I." The artists also use the "I" as a style to speak about how they represent the collective; they represent the people, the streets, and sometimes even the ugliness of society. They also use this as a method to stand distinct from the collective. This technique is a way for the rapper to embody the intellectual and social critic. The use of this technique has recently been the cause of much controversy among many of the underground artists. Several hip-hop artists have a song following the "I am . . ." pattern and each claims it as his own original innovation.[11] Because creativity and originality are so highly valued, claiming ownership of this idea allows the artists to position themselves as more talented or more authentic than the others. Thus, there is a high value on innovation, and the battle over who owns the "I" is an important site for the struggle over symbolic capital. The following is an excerpt from one of the "I" songs:

> *I'm the eye that sees; I'm the tongue that speaks;*
> *I'm the microphone that raises your voice;*
> *I'm the speaker that cancels out your silence;*
> *I'm the soul that died for you;*
> *I'm the voice that reaches you;*
> *I'm the eye that has seen injustice and has stayed silent for so long.*

The group Asfalt wrote this song in 2012.[12] In it, they use the "I" technique to position themselves as the voice of the people. It is clear that a song like this would appeal to those "revolutionary" fans who are the primary audience for all underground groups. These lines situate Asfalt as representative of the people; they claim they have been saying (through their music) what "the people" have wanted to say and expressing their feelings. In this way, Asfalt is not only saying they represent the people,

---

11 Chapter two provides a more in-depth discussion of the use of the "I," and I suggest there is continuity between the rappers' use of this technique and Salah Jahin's work from the mid-twentieth century.

12 The song title is "I Am Two Lines" (Ana Satrayn), which refers to "two lines" of the newspaper.

but also distinguishing themselves from them. Asfalt present themselves as being more capable of saying, doing, feeling, and expressing than "ordinary" people.

Asfalt released this song in September 2012. When it came out, four other artists from the underground scene posted songs they had created prior to this using the same "I am ..." pattern. Each artist claimed ownership of the idea and accused Asfalt of stealing it. By attacking Asfalt's creativity and authenticity, these artists claimed to be the more authentic rappers and positioned their identities in relation to others in the field. Additionally, the artists used their social capital through their alliances to support their claims, as there was no proof of which artist originally created this technique (although Asfalt was the only group to release a music video). Other rappers started to insult Asfalt and make accusations about how they came up with the idea (a technique known as 'dissing').[13] The "dis" battle began and all sorts of claims were being thrown back and forth on Facebook. A rapper named Abyusif was the most vocal about claiming to have invented the "I am . . ." form; he even recorded a "dis" track making fun of the members of Asfalt, asserting they are only pretending to be rappers, and saying that they have no real skills or talent. Abyusif, who has a significantly smaller fan base than Asfalt, used this situation as an attempt to accumulate greater legitimacy. Although his audience is smaller, Abyusif has strong social relationships with many of the artists in the underground scene and used these relationships to legitimate his claims. Another rapper, a member of Arabian Knightz, posted the following comment on Abyusif's artist page on Facebook: "Altay[14] one of my favorite rappers from Egypt and Arabia ... it's a shame such a BIG name group like asfalt couldn't create a hit without STEALING ur idea."[15] Support from other rappers shows Abyusif's social capital. After several rappers posted similar comments, Abyusif attempted to use this battle to paint himself as the underdog who produces original ideas. He posted several

---

13 The rappers in the underground community appropriate this slang English term and use it as an Egyptian Colloquial term; for example one might say *huwwa bydisak* ('he is dissing you').

14 Abyusif's given name.

15 A rapper copied and sent this comment to me from Abyusif's Facebook page. Abyusif removed it shortly after the resolution of the situation.

new tracks addressing this battle and even claimed that the members of Asfalt admitted to "being inspired" by his "I" song. According to Abyusif, this meant he "won" the battle. By asserting he was the "owner" of the "I am . . ." technique, he tried to form his identity as one of the most creative and original rappers, which would add to his symbolic capital. However, Asfalt took a different position and pointed out that there were several songs in the underground scene that use this technique, in order to prove that the idea belongs to no one. Thus, the battle ended with no gains for anyone.

Introducing the 'Rapper Self.' To further examine how the hip-hop artists in the underground scene form their identities through their music, I present an example of a song called "This Is My Life." Rappers Zap Tharwat and Mazagangy released this song in 2010. It exemplifies how "music seems to be key to identity because it offers, so intensely, a sense of both self and others, of the subjective in the collective" (Frith 1996:110).

They labeled me a terrorist, called me a butcher.
This is the first time I'm not talking about politics,
I'm going to explode.
I've opened up the door to my life, please come in.
I'll show you my qualities, it's about time for my arrival.
Arrival, arrival, for all the attendees.
Arrival, arrival, for all the listeners.
I go to a private university (right), electrical engineering (right),
Where I don't understand a thing (right), my life is flipping upside down (right).
Prisoner in my own country, president of the oppressed.
Our country is the poorest country, now you know why I'm depressed?
My age is counted by years, but with a mind like mine, I'm immortal.
November 1987 on the ledger, I'm a Muslim, a person of the book.
My country is Egypt, the country of goodness and torture.
My name is Ahmed Tharwat and Zap is my rap name.

This is my life, this is my world,

These are my problems and my worries, so what should I do?

Muslim, Arab, Egyptian, from Cairo,
Specifically from Shubra,
I'll tell you my story.
My hobby is rap, Mazagangy is my rap name.
Yes, I'm in my third year of high school; yes, I study humanities.
There's a new minister of culture, so I better be polite.
When I first started rapping, I felt depressed.
When people asked, "Why aren't your pants sagging and where is your hat?"
"Where's the gun and holster?"
"Where's your grey hair from preaching about the youth?"
"Where is the cussing and cursing?"
So I want to know, what am I supposed to do?
Mind my own business? Then why am I rapping?
They said, don't talk about big subjects, you'll forget with time.
"Of course this isn't a threat; it's only out of kindness."
So I said I'll take it easy, bit by bit,
But I won't listen to anyone who tells me to calm down.
Zap and I rap like the good book says.
It's not because we speak the truth that you describe us as terrorists.

Zap told me he wanted this song to be personal so that listeners could get to know the "real" him. Prior to writing this song, Zap had released several songs dealing with his political concerns, such as the US government's dealings with the Arab world and his take on Palestine. He told me that while talking to other hip-hop artists in the underground scene, they told him that he should write a song in which he introduces himself and includes personal information because "that's what rappers do."[16] Zap felt he needed to follow these expectations; he was not trying to copy other rappers, but he realized that he must follow a certain set of practices.

The translated song above starts with the line "They labeled me a terrorist, called me a butcher," which some people may interpret as

---

16 Conversation with Ahmed Tharwat, May 2012.

a reference to Westerners' stereotypes of Arabs.[17] However, Zap was commenting on his own personal experiences. Before becoming a well-known name in the underground hip-hop scene, he aspired to be a shaykh and studied *da'wa* (preaching Islam). Once he realized this path required intense commitment and studying, he decided it was not the direction he wanted to take. He still felt it was important to get his messages out to his community and he felt he could do this through rap. For Zap, this was still a form of *da'wa* in that he could spread moral and spiritual knowledge through a different medium. When he first started rapping, Zap had a beard, which inspired critique of his appearance as an "Islamist." The "butcher" comment is actually about his rapping skills; while people did not really respond to his look when he started, they could not deny his flow—he "slaughtered" the other rappers because his rhymes were so original and intelligently written. The song goes on to present the listeners with personal information about himself; his birthday, religion, name, and rap name. He claims that this is the first time he is not speaking about politics (in his music) and says that he will "explode" because of this. Here he is positioning himself as a person who actively critiques politics; he is informing his listeners that this is indeed an important aspect of his identity.

The next verse comes from rapper Mazagangy. He is a young rapper who has only been a part of the scene for a few years and is a member of the group Hip-Hop Project.[18] His verse gives further evidence of Egyptian rappers in the underground scene forming multiple collective identities through their music. By throwing out the words "Muslim," "Arab," and "Egyptian" in the first line, Mazagangy tells his listeners that he belongs to these three groups. The song "This Is My Life" addresses the problems and issues the individual rappers face; however, the use of

---

17 When I showed this music video to a mixed group of Americans and Egyptians (and translated the lyrics for non-Arabic speakers), the Americans all interpreted Zap's statement as a comment about how the "West" might stereotype Muslims and Arabs. They thought he was certainly addressing some Westerners' perceptions of Muslims being terrorists and Arabs being ignorant. Zap laughed when I told him this and he said this was not at all what he had in mind when he wrote the statement.

18 Hip-Hop Project consists of ten college-aged musicians who state on their Facebook page that they are "the first live Egyptian hip-hop band . . . a combination of guitars, drums, beat box, rappers, and vocals." Rappers Ali Loka and 3afreet, beat-boxer Hatem, and R&B singer Dalia Omar accompany Mazagangy in this group. I categorize them as Entertainers.

these three categories implies that Muslims, Arabs, and Egyptians have some shared experiences. Mazagangy does not need to explain further; the listeners should understand because he is situating himself as "one of them." The song goes on to speak about the misconceptions people have about rappers. By listing traits that are commonly associated with Western hip-hop artists (sagging pants, guns, cursing), Mazagangy is forming his identity by letting the audience know what "type" of rapper he is and complicating the common assumption of what it means to be a rapper. He does not have to participate in those sorts of practices in order to be a rapper; he is a rapper who uses this form of expression to "speak the truth."

The Hip-Hop Artist as an Agent of Change

Egyptian hip-hop artists position themselves as agents of social change; they are (or view themselves as) revolutionaries, political activists (or 'raptivists'),[19] and intellectuals. Rappers in the underground scene often rap about, and discuss through various venues, politics, issues of social justice, and morality.

The revolutionary rapper or the rapper as a political activist emerges as core to the identity of hip-hop artists cross-culturally. Literature on hip-hop in the Middle East and North Africa often focuses on how hip-hop artists use their music to address social and political issues, oppression, and struggle. In Kahf's work on Arabic hip-hop as a new genre, he examines this musical form as an "emancipatory and empowering avenue of expression" (2007:359). Hip-hop is often associated with freedom of expression and it allows artists space to "participate in the public discourse of their society" (2007:359). Morgan and Bennett point out, "In North Africa, where young people played a central role in the national protest movements, hip-hop emerged as the music of free speech and political resistance" (2011:178). Also, these scholars suggest that we should consider "hip-hop to be the lingua franca for popular and political youth culture around the world" (2011:179).

---

19 'Raptivist' is a term some of the artists use to describe what they do: activism through rap. Artists have only recently started using this term. I believe it comes from a special project in which some of them participated in Denmark in October 2012 called RAPOLITICS, in which the sponsoring organization referred to these artists using the term 'raptivist.'

While it is valuable to consider how rappers use hip-hop as a form of opposition, there are other factors that contribute to the formation of hip-hop artists' revolutionary and activist messages. The field of hip-hop in Egypt, specifically in times of social and political upheaval, requires that the rapper address specific issues. While some of the artists in the underground scene were discussing politics prior to the revolution, others shifted their focus considerably to keep up with the field's trends. I argue here that some artists are "riding the wave of the revolution," or taking part in opportunistic nationalism in order to maintain legitimacy in the field. Benjamin Geer suggests that "individuals who are seen as embodying religious or nationalist ideals" have the potential to gain "power and prestige" (2012:18). In line with this idea, I posit that as the demands of the field shifted, the hip-hop artists kept up with these demands so as to gain or maintain their symbolic capital, regardless of their "true" beliefs. Thus, identity shapes and is shaped by the field.

As an intellectual, the rapper asserts that he has a perspective on social and political issues that others do not. The rapper as an intellectual often addresses issues pertaining to morality and spirituality. He discusses why drugs are "bad" and wearing a headscarf is "good." Artists often provide daily posts on their Facebook pages of insightful, poetic, and inspirational thoughts to share their knowledge with the public. This is a crucial point for examining how the artists actively mold their identities as intellectuals. An interesting aspect of viewing the hip-hop artist as the intellectual has been how the "public" has cited the artists' work as cause for protesting or used the artists' lyrics in protests.[20] If the rapper's audience views him as an intellectual, this particular part of the artist's subjectivity could deepen. We can see examples of how rappers position themselves as intellectuals in the statements they write on their Facebook pages. They make statements such as "I am the voice of the Arab people,"[21] "I am considered [to be] the voice of wisdom,"[22] and "My purpose is to provide pure, inspirational, revolutionary poetry."[23] These statements are made within the greater context of the individual forming his identity as a rapper; rappers can make these sorts of statements

---

20   I provide an example of this in chapter two.
21   Shobokshy.
22   Zap Tharwat.
23   Aly Talibab.

while "ordinary" people cannot. Thus they are participating in a process of distinction by claiming "authority" to speak for the people and separating themselves from the "ordinary."

We cannot view the hip-hop artist as a revolutionary, an activist, and an intellectual as existing completely separately; rather they are facets of identity imbricated into one another. For example, addressing the Palestinian question allows the rapper to simultaneously perform as all three. Discussing Palestine is an opportunity for the rappers to inform, appeal to morality, and urge people to mobilize for a cause. The song "Who's the Target?" is a good example of rappers situating themselves as agents of social change. Zap Tharwat, Ibrahim Farouk, and Gad Kareem released it on YouTube in December 2011.

> *A true story beginning with a salute: "Peace be upon you" to everyone in the Arab nation;*
> *The salute ends at the beginning of the song.*
> *It's the same story with a little variation.*
> *2008 he was addressing the Jews.*
> *$30 billion to make soldiers.*
> *His words were clear, filled with promises.*
> *Just reaching presidency, Hamas kicked off.*
> *How can we believe someone who is always changing their tune?*
> *Today he's on my side, tomorrow I'll be his enemy.*
> *Let me speak even if afterwards I die—*
> *I'll die but I won't die in silence.*
> *Jerusalem is Arab, Gaza is Arab, the West Bank is Arab, Haifa is Arab.*
> *Shame on you, Arabs, to give in to humiliation*
> *And let your life be ruled by Americans.*
>
> *Who's the target? Me, my religion, or my country?*
> *My mother, my sister, or my children?*
> *I'm calling out in the loudest voice I have, I'm calling out;*
> *I'm telling you that you have no right to enslave me.*
>
> *We often see Muslims taken to trial; we're called ignorant and religion is always blamed.*

The Hip-Hop Artist as an Agent of Change

"Arabs are ignorant, spending money left and right."
Look who's talking; it's an American entrapment.
Bin Laden was blamed for all that was destroyed.
Please tell me, who will pay for Palestine?
Iraq, Lebanon, Kashmir, Afghanistan, Iran, Sudan. ("Tell me more, Gad!")
The Twin Towers were destroyed
And the embassy planted the idea among us, all the drama, and vote for "Mubarak, Obama."
Porn invaded our culture, and we all imitated it.
We care for nothing but our earthly needs.
They're taking our land,
We're being harassed,
They're killing our people—
Where are our rights?
But as long as there's one God, one dream, one goal, we'll always be number one.

Who said burning the Qur'an will solve our problems?
Arabs have been beaten and killed for so long.
How many families slept under ashes just so they can live?
Too many lies have been told, scenarios have been repeated,
All for the sake of justice, freedom, and reformation of the Arab nation!
Our Arab nation must speak out, no more silence.
My question right now is, who is the target?

This song is a clear representation of the common themes found in the underground Egyptian hip-hop scene. Reviewing songs written by these specific artists prior to the revolution,[24] it is clear that they were rapping about their personal problems (such as attaining university education and employment), rather than about nationalism, political resistance, and moral issues such as Palestine and pornography as they do in this example. By addressing these issues, these artists immediately

---

24 I speak of two of the three artists; the primary themes of the third artist's music had always been centered on these issues.

became among the most popular artists in the scene.[25] This song seems to represent the formula for success in the underground scene after the revolution. However, the artists claim they wrote this song prior to the revolution in order to avoid being categorized as rappers who used specific themes to gain popularity.[26] They position their identities as being real activists, revolutionaries, and intellectuals. The political climate indeed influences the emphasis on these specific portrayals of identity. I believe that the artists use the temporal marker of the revolution as way to sustain legitimacy (or symbolic capital).

However, there are examples of songs that addressed revolutionary ideas prior to the revolution. For example, the song titled "Writing a Letter for Tomorrow" was released on YouTube on January 23, 2011, two days prior to the revolution. During the following days people wrote saying they were encouraged to protest after listening to this song, and subsequently joined other Egyptians in Tahrir Square. Below is a selection from the song, written by Zap Tharwat:

Afraid of pain, beaten by a whip that leaves its mark on our minds.
I exist and I don't exist, living without a voice.
They can hear me and they laugh, all while buying my death.
This country never listens—so my letter is in my coffin.
I'm writing a letter for tomorrow, afraid it will never arrive,
Because words in our country never reach.

Temporal positioning is a key component to gaining symbolic capital in the field. The author of "Writing a Letter for Tomorrow" has proof that he was writing about politics prior to the revolution. He is much respected among his peers and is rarely accused of "riding the wave of the revolution" as other artists are. While some rappers' identities have clearly fluctuated in times of revolution, rappers and other musicians in the underground music scene respect their peers who show the most

---

25 In fact, the song is still a huge hit in the scene. I have seen the artists perform it many times and the audience goes crazy every time. I think this song is one of the reasons these rappers book more concerts than any other rappers in the scene.

26 I know that at least one verse from the song existed prior to the revolution, as it appears in an earlier song by the same artist. However, other rappers in the field have told me that they believe the other two artists are "riding the wave" and using these themes to gain popularity.

consistent portrayal of identity and view them as the most legitimate. Zap has managed to gain and maintain symbolic capital by portraying a consistent identity. Since consistency and involvement in revolutionary activities or speaking against hegemonic powers are crucial to the rapper's identity, much effort goes into proving and maintaining this image.

"You Are Not Appearing as Yourself": Identity and the Market

Just as particular feelings of identification with various identities transform and shift within specific social contexts, attachments to individual aspects of one's identity are also unstable and inconsistent. The market factors into and disrupts the identity formation of Egyptian rappers.

Ibrahim and Gad are well-known rappers in the underground scene. They generally follow the rules of the field; they write their own lyrics and stick to the popular topics. Ahmad Mikki, a popular Egyptian actor and mainstream rapper, asked them to participate in a commercial for a brand of potato chips. They agreed to be in the advertisement, although they were not appearing as themselves, but rather as stereotypical "Western" hip-hop artists (baggy pants, big necklaces, baseball caps) rapping lyrics written by a major corporation.

I have argued earlier that artists in the underground scene are competing for symbolic capital. Bourdieu describes the accumulation of symbolic capital in the artistic world as an eventual guarantee of economic profits that relies on the misrecognition of the artists' intentions of seeking economic rewards for their art. The artistic community must perceive the artists as doing "art for art's sake" in order for the artists to gain symbolic capital, which will later lead to economic capital (Bourdieu 1993:75).

Based on the story of Ibrahim, Gad, and the commercial, I depart from Bourdieu's emphasis on the necessity of this misrecognition to gain symbolic capital. Some hip-hop artists considered their participation in this advertisement campaign as a reinforcement of their legitimacy as artists, as opposed to a "selling out" for economic gain. Thus, economic gain and artistic legitimacy may not be as strongly opposed, in this context, as Bourdieu insists. In the case of these rappers, their peers in the underground scene could categorize them as sell-outs (they sold their "creative" selves). However, they were chosen by the only mainstream rapper in Egypt to participate in the campaign. Although they were clearly seeking economic gain or popularity (both of which oppose the rules of the artistic field), most of the artists view this situation as a symbolic gain which in fact reinforces these rappers' identities as legitimate rappers.[27] When I questioned other rappers about this—as these actions seem to go against the values of the field—they expressed the opinion that if any rapper told me they would not accept the same opportunity they would be lying. In this case, the content of the advertisement, the silly outfits, and the fact that the rappers did not write their own lyrics were not as important as the fact that someone of status (the mainstream rapper) *chose* them over all other rappers. This in itself was validation of the rappers' skills; this validation seemed to override the fact that members of the hip-hop scene might usually look down upon this sort of activity. Here, Bourdieu's assertion that "activities and resources gain in symbolic power, or legitimacy, to the extent that they become separated from underlying material interests and hence go misrecognized as representing disinterested forms of activities and resources" does not apply (Swartz 1997:90). These rappers were able to accumulate more symbolic capital, in the form of recognition and prestige, because of their participation in the advertisement. While Bourdieu's theories are applicable to "high culture" in France, they do not address the way the cultural field works in different contexts. It must be recognized that the underground Egyptian hip-hop scene works under different rules, and artists can sometimes shed aspects of their constructed identities in pursuit of economic capital without necessarily risking their symbolic capital. This works specifically when the symbolic capital at stake is recognition.

On the sidelines. The "market" does not refer only to big corporations, which play a role in shaping cultural work. There is a market for every field, including the underground hip-hop scene. While these artists are viscerally opposed to mainstream Egyptian music and assert that the artists who make popular music do not use their own ideas, the market for revolutionary music also controls production in the underground scene. The artists who are popular write about what their fans like to listen to—politics and revolution. However, there is one rapper, Aly Talibab, who

---

27 Of course I must generalize here. There were a few rappers with whom I spoke who said they would never participate in this sort of campaign.

does not appear to be greatly influenced by the market. I claim that Aly Talibab is the most autonomous rapper in the field, because he has created a space for himself to follow his own rules, rather than the rules of the field. As I discussed earlier, the rapper as a revolutionary is a major value of the field; not only does the rapper need to rap about revolutionary ideas, but he also must participate in revolutionary activities. Talibab's participation is never in question, as he does not make any claims or produce music centered on these ideas. He does not appear in interviews discussing his revolutionary activities, so other rappers cannot accuse him of "riding the wave." By not addressing the major issues and topics of the field, he does not allow room for other artists to question his legitimacy. Talibab does not have to prove anything. He stays on the sideline of the field where he can still participate but does not get too involved.

Aly Talibab also has an "I" song. While many artists use this style to assert their identity as being either one of the people, the voice of the people, or a voice of wisdom, Talibab uses it to speak about the ugliness of people and society. His song is a social critique about his own practices and of others around him. Rather than taking on the common "voice of the people" role, it seems Talibab is saying that, because he is part of society, he is part of the problem; everyone is part of the problem, everyone contributes. A few lines from Talibab's 2012 song "Perfection" express this idea.

> *I'm the anger I couldn't control.*
> *I'm the ignorance, the shit that I talk and the things I pretend.*
> *I'm the generation, the Americanized, the smart ass, the complicated, the blindfolded.*

The market does not seem to greatly influence Talibab's identity formation. He does not follow the trends of most of the other rap songs, which are most certainly products of the market for this specific type of music. As previously indicated, in times of revolution Egyptian nationalism and pan-Arabism have gained popularity and hip-hop artists have increased their use of nationalist themes in their music—what I refer to as an "opportunistic nationalism." Talibab, on the other hand, does not use these themes in his music; in fact he even put up a post on Facebook declaring, "Fuck you, nationalism, we are all earthlings," which clearly opposes what the underground market is calling for. While he definitely writes lyrics that I would categorize as political opposition and social critique, he does not do it in a way that would appeal to the market for this type of music; people want to hear about how they are good and the government is bad. Talibab is an example of a hip-hop artist whose creative identity overpowers other aspects of his identity as a hip-hop artist. For him, the "industry" of producing music never played a role in his musical or lyrical choice. He attempts to stay as far away as possible from this part of the scene because he realizes that when he starts producing music for money, the content will be—at least to some extent—dictated by what consumers want.[28] He removes himself from the field as much as possible while still participating in it. This is in part due to the fact that he, possibly more than any other artist, is not concerned with consumers. He makes music because he likes to.

Thus, it is evident that the market can sometimes mold the artists' identities. Artists are willing to portray themselves according to the demands of the market, while the ways in which the artists represent themselves also shape the market for Egyptian hip-hop.

Conclusion

The identity formation of Egyptian underground hip-hop artists, through practices, songs, and self-representation, reveal how cultural products can act as a crucial site for studying identity as a process of "becoming" rather than "being." The bodily practices Egyptian rappers use to *feel* like rappers depict this process. The ways in which subjective and collective identities fluctuate in the Egyptian hip-hop scene also reveal identity as a process. While the artists' feelings, experiences, and representations of themselves are indeed formed within the context of a specific time and space, they also take part in creating the "tradition" of Egyptian rap. Egyptian hip-hop, a relatively new form of cultural

---

28 During a conversation with Talibab, I realized that his entire principle of creating music for the sake of music developed when he first started rapping in 2007. He informed me that during this time no rappers in Egypt were making money from their music, so he did not even consider this to be an option. Talibab, unlike the others, never made the shift to the goal of producing music for money. It is not that he is particularly wealthy and thus has the luxury of making music without being concerned with money. He worked at a call center during the time of my research and informed me he felt it was best to keep music as a hobby.

Conclusion

expression, has its own rules and values; the artists in the scene have collectively formed what it means to be a "legitimate" or "authentic" rapper. Therefore, as more artists join the scene, they will in turn form their identities as "Egyptian rappers" by taking these values into consideration. Thus, it is clear that identity shapes and is shaped by particular fields. Moreover, the struggle over valuable resources or symbolic capital, such as honor, prestige, and recognition, contributes to identity formation in the underground scene, as each artist strives to be the "ideal rapper." The pursuit of symbolic capital sometimes results in the artists emphasizing specific aspects of their identities. Additionally, we must consider the role of the market in identity formation, as it reveals that attachments to particular aspects of one's identity are negotiable while others are not. While this chapter has served as a critical examination of how Egyptian hip-hop acts as a site of identity formation among the artists in the scene, it would be worthwhile to explore how cultural products from times of upheaval and change contribute to the identity formation of consumers as well.

CHAPTER 6

Conclusion

This monograph is an ethnographic exploration of Egyptian rappers and their practices and has examined the multiple ways in which the underground hip-hop scene acts as a site of struggle. Through a close examination of song lyrics, interviews, and the interactions of the cultural workers in the scene, it is evident that Egyptian rappers are collaboratively molding a new form of cultural expression in Egypt. While the artists collectively agree that they are participating in the hip-hop "movement," they vary in the way they locate, emphasize, and embody their social and cultural roles.

Egyptian rappers struggle to define their positions in the canonical music scene in Egypt. As we saw in chapter two, this leads the rappers to turn to the use of narratives to explain the emergence of this musical genre. These problematic narratives either focus on attempting to link rap to "traditional" Arab practices or they reflect the notion that hip-hop is a Western import that requires nurturing before it is ready to enter the mainstream Egyptian music scene. These narratives often overlook the continuities between the work of rappers and other Egyptian cultural products from the twentieth century. These continuities express themselves in a variety of fascinating forms, such as the sampling of earlier Egyptian songs, references to oppositional musicians, the blending of humor and critique, and the use of techniques created by earlier cultural workers. By exploring these continuities, this thesis draws attention to the unique qualities of this new form of cultural expression.

With this form of expression, Egyptian hip-hop artists articulate multifaceted degrees of opposition. As outlined in chapter three, this opposition is largely centered on discontent with social and political circumstances. Artists use their lyrics to inform people of the realities of society and place the blame on both the government and ordinary people for these unfortunate realities. Simultaneously, rappers attempt to offer optimistic outlooks on life by urging people to imagine alternative ways of living. While the majority of lyrics in the underground hip-hop scene are seemingly oppositional, they also reveal that "opposition" has several layers, and in many ways rappers are only beginning to question dominant attitudes and ideology. Upon close analysis we can see that their music is imbued with reinforcing popular notions concerning class and gender. Understanding the artists and their practices requires the disentangling of "hip-hop" and "opposition."

In that sense, it is also critical to understand that these rappers care about creating a consumable and enjoyable product and that rap is not only about the message. Chapter four's exploration of the rappers' conceptions of 'good art' points to ways in which they embody their aesthetic preferences in their artistic practices. They present their knowledge, skills, and fashion as assertions that they are "in the know" in the underground scene, and this is a major means of gaining and maintaining subcultural capital. The production of 'good rap' is of critical importance to these rappers on multiple levels. Their concern with making 'good' music rests in the desire to appeal to an audience and convey their messages effectively. They often diverge in their conceptions of what it means to be a 'good rapper,' which leads them to situate themselves among others who share similar preferences and differentiate themselves from those who do not.

Egyptian rappers in the underground scene shape their identities through various modes. Chapter five explains that they simultaneously desire to present themselves as the "ideal hip-hop artist" and to *feel* like a rapper. They engage in extensive training, such as repeated movement, in order to cultivate an inner sense of a 'rapper self.' This type of training points to the use of external bodily practices as a means of forming an inner disposition. In order to ensure that others in the field of Egyptian hip-hop view them as artists, they participate in various practices such as naming and self-assertions. These techniques allow the artists to represent themselves as revolutionaries, activists, intellectuals, and political critics. We can view these representations as a reflection of a positioning to gain valuable assets in the field, such as fame, recognition, and prestige. These are all forms of symbolic capital. They also use their social capital to support their claims of authenticity, originality, and legitimacy.

Bibliography

Abbas, Basel. 2005. "An Analysis of Arabic Hip Hop." PhD dissertation, SAE Institute London.
Abdel-Malek, Kamal. 1990. *The Study of the Vernacular Poetry of Ahmad Fu'ad Nigm*. Leiden: E.J. Brill.
Alim, H. Samy. 2009. *Global Linguistic Flows: Hip Hop Cultures, Youth Identities and the Politics of Language*. New York: Routledge.
Armbrust, Walter. 1996. *Mass Culture and Modernism in Egypt*. Cambridge: Cambridge University Press.
Bennet, Andy. 1999. "Hip Hop am Main: The Localization of Rap Music and Hip Hop Culture," *Media, Culture, & Society*, 21: 77–91.
Bourdieu, Pierre. 1986. "The Forms of Capital." In J. Richardson, ed. *Handbook of Theory and Research for the Sociology of Education*, 241–258. New York: Greenwood, 1986.
———. 1993. *The Field of Cultural Production: Essays on Art and Literature*, edited by Randal Johnson. Cambridge: Polity Press.
Erll, Astrid. 2011. *Memory in Culture*, translated by Sara B. Young. New York: Palgrave Macmillan.
Fahmy, Ziad. 2011. *Ordinary Egyptians*. Stanford: Stanford University Press.
Frith, Simon. 1996. "Music and Identity." In Stuart Hall and Paul du Gay, eds. *Questions of Cultural Identity*, 108–127. London: SAGE Publications.
Geer, Benjamin. 2012. "The Priesthood of Nationalism in Egypt: Duty, Authority, Autonomy." PhD dissertation, University of London.
Hall, Stuart. 1996. "Introduction: Who Needs 'Identity.'" In Stuart Hall and Paul du Gay, eds. *Questions of Cultural Identity*, 1–17. London: SAGE Publications.

El Hamamsy, Walid, and Mounira Soliman. 2013. "Introduction: Popular Culture—A Site of Resistance." In Walid El Hamamsy and Mounira Soliman, eds. *Popular Culture in the Middle East and North Africa: A Postcolonial Outlook*, 1–14. New York: Routledge.

Hebdige, Dick. 1979. *Subculture: The Meaning of Style*. London: Routledge.

Hindi, Khalil. 1979. "Profile: Ahmed Fouad Negm," *Index on Censorship*, 8: 50–51.

Jahin, Salah. 1963. *Rubaiyat Salah Jahin*. Cairo: The Egyptian General Authority for Books and National Documents.

Kahf, Usama. 2007. "Arabic Hip Hop: Claim of Authenticity and Identity of a New Genre," *Journal of Popular Music Studies*, 19(4): 359–385.

Khouri, Mounah. 1971. *Poetry and the Making of Modern Egypt (1882–1922)*. Leiden: E.J. Brill.

Lizardo, Omar, and Sara Skiles. 2008. "Cultural Consumption in the Fine and Popular Arts Realms," *Sociology Compass*, 2: 485–502.

Maguadda, Paola. 2009. "Processes of Institutionalization and 'Symbolic Struggles' in the 'Independent Music' Field in Italy," *Modern Italy*, 14: 295–310.

Mahmood, Saba. 2005. *Politics of Piety*. Princeton: Princeton University Press.

Morgan, Marcyliena, and Dionne Bennett. 2011. "Hip-Hop and the Global Imprint of a Black Cultural Form," *The Journal of the American Academy of Arts and Sciences*, 140(2): 176–196.

Radwan, Noha. 2012. *Egyptian Colloquial Poetry in the Modern Arabic Canon*. New York: Palgrave Macmillan.

Saad, Reem. 2012. "The Egyptian Revolution: A Triumph of Poetry," *American Ethnologist*, 39: 63–66.

Salaam, Mtume ya. 1995. "The Aesthetics of Rap," *African American Review*, 29: 303–315.

Shusterman, Richard. 1991. "The Fine Art of Rap," *New Literary History*, 22: 613–632.

Swartz, David. 1997. *Culture and Power: The Sociology of Pierre Bourdieu*. Chicago: University of Chicago Press.

Swedenburg, Ted. 2013. "Palestinian Rap: Against the Struggle Paradigm." In Walid El Hamamsy and Mounira Soliman, eds. *Popular*

Bibliography

Culture in the Middle East and North Africa: A Postcolonial Outlook, 17–32. New York: Routledge.

Terkourafi, Marina. 2010. *Languages of Global Hip-Hop*. London: Continuum International Publishing.

Tharwat, Ahmed. 2012. *Poetic Attempts: Agenda*. Cairo: Dar Diwan.

Thorton, Sarah. 2006. "Understanding Hipness: 'Subcultural Capital' as Feminist Tool." In Andy Bennett, Barry Shank, and Jason Toynbee, eds. *The Popular Music Studies Reader*, 99–105. London: Routledge.

Williams, Angela. 2010. "We Ain't Terrorists but We Droppin' Bombs: Language Use and Localization in Egyptian Hip Hop." In Marina Terkourafi, ed. *Languages of Global Hip-Hop*, 67–95. London: Continuum International Publishing.

Williams, Raymond. 1976. *Keywords: A Vocabulary of Culture and Society*. New York: Oxford University Press.

Songs

Abyusif. 2007. "A French Song."

Ahmad Mikki. 2012. Introduction to the album *Originally Arab*. Melody Music. http://www.youtube.com/watch?v=eJ50Nlb-YC4&list=PLCB430437E5B46199

Aly Talibab. 2011. "Perfection." http://www.youtube.com/watch?v=cRPjUl1zVTU

Arabian Knightz. 2013. "We Are the Government." http://www.youtube.com/watch?v=1mya9bh85mU

Asfalt. 2009. "Guys at Cafés."

Asfalt. 2009. "I Want."

Asfalt. 2012. "I Am Two Lines." http://www.youtube.com/watch?v=JfRmi3ssDEc

Asfalt and Zap Tharwat. 2011. "Who's the Target." http://www.youtube.com/watch?v=wKiWuW4Off4

Cairokee. 2012. "We Are the People." Written by 'Abd al-Rahman al-Adnudi. http://www.youtube.com/watch?v=d6dlzIZbW4g

Cairokee featuring Zap Tharwat. 2012. "Stand Your Ground." http://www.youtube.com/watch?v=rYoCS7i0SIg&list=PLA6F845D9D258E864&index=17

Deeb. 2011. "Stand Up, Egyptian." http://deeb.bandcamp.com/track/feat-edd-prod-by-edd-2

Deeb. 2012. "Destined." http://deeb.bandcamp.com/track/prod-by-deeb-2
EL Zero, F Killa, MC Monadel, and Mr. Kordy. 2010. "Slums." http://www.youtube.com/watch?v=KA6XLWB5eB0
F Killa. 2012. "A Message to Every Harasser." http://www.youtube.com/watch?v=e6SMRcCnaBk
Haty. 2007. "Everything's Fine."
Ibrahim Farouk and Deeb. 2006. "*Al-'ebara fi al-'abara*."
MC Amin, Sphinx, E-Money, and F Killa. 2012. "Hey Morsi." http://www.youtube.com/watch?v=gbA3DfojxI0
MC Loser. 2008. "Searching."
Qusai, Rush, Balti, Ayzee, Vico, Flipp, Murder Eyez, Timz, and Talal. 2011. "Arab World Unite." http://www.youtube.com/watch?v=43wezG6MeGM
Sayyid Darwish. 1920? "Stand Up, Egyptian." http://www.youtube.com/watch?v=h4b2o1WYFOA I translated this song by listening to it from this YouTube link. Ziad Fahmy also provides a translation of Darwish's lyrics in *Ordinary Egyptians* (161); the translation I provide differs slightly. Fahmy's notes (216) state that this song was recorded by a record company and that the printed lyrics are located in *Makatabat al-Iskandariya* under Sayyid Darwish, vol. 2, 415–416.
Shobokshy. 2012. "Sons of Bitches." http://www.youtube.com/watch?v=3tiBf02H2pc&list=UU3EeLcfpUSX-lGkXISavSTQ&index=27
Zap Tharwat. 2009. "Obama." http://www.youtube.com/watch?v=zMWW2jI-bI4
Zap Tharwat and Mazagangy. 2010. "This Is My Life." http://www.youtube.com/watch?v=6jmBJr28ShY
Zap Tharwat. 2011. "Writing a Letter for Tomorrow."
Zap Tharwat. 2012. "How Many." http://www.youtube.com/watch?v=38MnBmuyUzU

About the Author

Ellen R. Weis has an MA in Middle East Studies from the American University in Cairo. This manuscript is based on her MA thesis.

CAIRO PAPERS IN SOCIAL SCIENCE

Volume One
1   *Women, Health and Development,* Cynthia Nelson, ed.
2   *Democracy in Egypt,* Ali E. Hillal Dessouki, ed.
3   *Mass Communications and the October War,* Olfat Hassan Agha
4   *Rural Resettlement in Egypt,* Helmy Tadros
5   *Saudi Arabian Bedouin,* Saad E. Ibrahim and Donald P. Cole

Volume Two
1   *Coping With Poverty in a Cairo Community,* Andrea B. Rugh
2   *Modernization of Labor in the Arab Gulf,* Enid Hill
3   *Studies in Egyptian Political Economy,* Herbert M. Thompson
4   *Law and Social Change in Contemporary Egypt,* Cynthia Nelson and Klaus Friedrich Koch, eds.
5   *The Brain Drain in Egypt,* Saneya Saleh

Volume Three
1   *Party and Peasant in Syria,* Raymond Hinnebusch
2   *Child Development in Egypt,* Nicholas V. Ciaccio
3   *Living Without Water,* Asaad Nadim et al.
4   *Export of Egyptian School Teachers,* Suzanne A. Messiha
5   *Population and Urbanization in Morocco,* Saad E. Ibrahim

Volume Four
1   *Cairo's Nubian Families,* Peter Geiser
2, 3 *Symposium on Social Research for Development: Proceedings,* Social Research Center
4   *Women and Work in the Arab World,* Earl L. Sullivan and Karima Korayem

Volume Five
1   *Ghagar of Sett Guiranha: A Study of a Gypsy Community in Egypt,* Nabil Sobhi Hanna
2   *Distribution of Disposal Income and the Impact of Eliminating Food Subsidies in Egypt,* Karima Korayem
3   *Income Distribution and Basic Needs in Urban Egypt,* Amr Mohie el-Din

Volume Six
1   *The Political Economy of Revolutionary Iran*, Mihssen Kadhim
2   *Urban Research Strategies in Egypt*, Richard A. Lobban, ed.
3   *Non-alignment in a Changing World*, Mohammed el-Sayed Selim, ed.
4   *The Nationalization of Arabic and Islamic Education in Egypt: Dar al-Alum and al-Azhar*, Lois A. Arioan

Volume Seven
1   *Social Security and the Family in Egypt*, Helmi Tadros
2   *Basic Needs, Inflation and the Poor of Egypt*, Myrette el-Sokkary
3   *The Impact of Development Assistance On Egypt*, Earl L. Sullivan, ed.
4   *Irrigation and Society in Rural Egypt*, Sohair Mehanna, Richard Huntington, and Rachad Antonius

Volume Eight
1, 2   *Analytic Index of Survey Research in Egypt*, Madiha el-Safty, Monte Palmer, and Mark Kennedy

Volume Nine
1   *Philosophy, Ethics and Virtuous Rule*, Charles E. Butterworth
2   *The 'Jihad': An Islamic Alternative in Egypt*, Nemat Guenena
3   *The Institutionalization of Palestinian Identity in Egypt*, Maha A. Dajani
4   *Social Identity and Class in a Cairo Neighborhood*, Nadia A. Taher

Volume Ten
1   *Al-Sanhuri and Islamic Law*, Enid Hill
2   *Gone For Good*, Ralph Sell
3   *The Changing Image of Women in Rural Egypt*, Mona Abaza
4   *Informal Communities in Cairo: the Basis of a Typology*, Linda Oldham, Haguer el Hadidi, and Hussein Tamaa

Volume Eleven
1   *Participation and Community in Egyptian New Lands: The Case of South Tahrir*, Nicholas Hopkins et al.
2   *Palestinian Universities Under Occupation*, Antony T. Sullivan
3   *Legislating Infitah: Investment, Foreign Trade and Currency Laws*, Khaled M. Fahmy
4   *Social History of An Agrarian Reform Community in Egypt*, Reem Saad

Volume Twelve
1   *Cairo's Leap Forward: People, Households, and Dwelling Space,* Fredric Shorter
2   *Women, Water, and Sanitation: Household Water Use in Two Egyptian Villages,* Samiha el-Katsha et al.
3   *Palestinian Labor in a Dependent Economy: Women Workers in the West Bank Clothing Industry,* Randa Siniora
4   *The Oil Question in Egyptian-Israeli Relations, 1967–1979: A Study in International Law and Resource Politics,* Karim Wissa

Volume Thirteen
1   *Squatter Markets in Cairo,* Helmi R. Tadros, Mohamed Feteeha, and Allen Hibbard
2   *The Sub-culture of Hashish Users in Egypt: A Descriptive Analytic Study,* Nashaat Hassan Hussein
3   *Social Background and Bureaucratic Behavior in Egypt,* Earl L. Sullivan, el Sayed Yassin, Ali Leila, and Monte Palmer
4   *Privatization: the Egyptian Debate,* Mostafa Kamel el-Sayyid

Volume Fourteen
1   *Perspectives on the Gulf Crisis,* Dan Tschirgi and Bassam Tibi
2   *Experience and Expression: Life Among Bedouin Women in South Sinai,* Deborah Wickering
3   *Impact of Temporary International Migration on Rural Egypt,* Atef Hanna Nada
4   *Informal Sector in Egypt,* Nicholas S. Hopkins ed.

Volume Fifteen
1   *Scenes of Schooling: Inside a Girls' School in Cairo,* Linda Herrera
2   *Urban Refugees: Ethiopians and Eritreans in Cairo,* Dereck Cooper
3   *Investors and Workers in the Western Desert of Egypt: An Exploratory Survey,* Naeim Sherbiny, Donald Cole, and Nadia Makary
4   *Environmental Challenges in Egypt and the World,* Nicholas S. Hopkins, ed.

Volume Sixteen
1   *The Socialist Labor Party: A Case Study of a Contemporary Egyptian Opposition Party,* Hanaa Fikry Singer
2   *The Empowerment of Women: Water and Sanitation Initiatives in Rural Egypt,* Samiha el Katsha and Susan Watts
3   *The Economics and Politics of Structural Adjustment in Egypt: Third Annual Symposium*

4 *Experiments in Community Development in a Zabbaleen Settlement,* Marie Assaad and Nadra Garas

Volume Seventeen
1 *Democratization in Rural Egypt: A Study of the Village Local Popular Council,* Hanan Hamdy Radwan
2 *Farmers and Merchants: Background for Structural Adjustment in Egypt,* Sohair Mehanna, Nicholas S. Hopkins, and Bahgat Abdelmaksoud
3 *Human Rights: Egypt and the Arab World, Fourth Annual Symposium*
4 *Environmental Threats in Egypt: Perceptions and Actions,* Salwa S. Gomaa, ed.

Volume Eighteen
1 *Social Policy in the Arab World,* Jacqueline Ismael and Tareq Y. Ismael
2 *Workers, Trade Union and the State in Egypt: 1984–1989,* Omar el-Shafie
3 *The Development of Social Science in Egypt: Economics, History and Sociology; Fifth Annual Symposium*
4 *Structural Adjustment, Stabilization Policies and the Poor in Egypt,* Karima Korayem

Volume Nineteen
1 *Nilopolitics: A Hydrological Regime, 1870–1990,* Mohamed Hatem el-Atawy
2 *Images of the Other: Europe and the Muslim World Before 1700,* David R. Blanks et al.
3 *Grass Roots Participation in the Development of Egypt,* Saad Eddin Ibrahim et al.
4 *The Zabbalin Community of Muqattam,* Elena Volpi and Doaa Abdel Motaal

Volume Twenty
1 *Class, Family, and Power in an Egyptian Village,* Samer el-Karanshawy
2 *The Middle East and Development in a Changing World,* Donald Heisel, ed.
3 *Arab Regional Women's Studies Workshop,* Cynthia Nelson and Soraya Altorki, eds.
4 *"Just a Gaze": Female Clientele of Diet Clinics in Cairo: An Ethnomedical Study,* Iman Farid Bassyouny

Volume Twenty-one
1 *Turkish Foreign Policy During the Gulf War of 1990–1991,* Mostafa Aydin
2 *State and Industrial Capitalism in Egypt,* Samer Soliman

3   *Twenty Years of Development in Egypt (1977–1997): Part I*, Mark C. Kennedy
4   *Twenty Years of Development in Egypt (1977–1997): Part II*, Mark C. Kennedy

Volume Twenty-two
1   *Poverty and Poverty Alleviation Strategies in Egypt*, Ragui Assaad and Malak Rouchdy
2   *Between Field and Text: Emerging Voices in Egyptian Social Science*, Seteney Shami and Linda Hererra, eds.
3   *Masters of the Trade: Crafts and Craftspeople in Cairo, 1750–1850*, Pascale Ghazaleh
4   *Discourses in Contemporary Egypt: Politics and Social Issues*, Enid Hill, ed.

Volume Twenty-three
1   *Fiscal Policy Measures in Egypt: Public Debt and Food Subsidy*, Gouda Abdel-Khalek and Karima Korayem
2   *New Frontiers in the Social History of the Middle East*, Enid Hill, ed.
3   *Egyptian Encounters*, Jason Thompson, ed.
4   *Women's Perception of Environmental Change in Egypt*, Eman el Ramly

Volume Twenty-four
1, 2   *The New Arab Family*, Nicholas S. Hopkins, ed.
3   *An Investigation of the Phenomenon of Polygyny in Rural Egypt*, Laila S. Shahd
4   *The Terms of Empowerment: Islamic Women Activists in Egypt*, Sherine Hafez

Volume Twenty-five
1, 2   *Elections in the Middle East: What do they Mean?* Iman A. Hamdy, ed.
3   *Employment Crisis of Female Graduates in Egypt: An Ethnographic Account*, Ghada F. Barsoum
4   *Palestinian and Israeli Nationalism: Identity Politics and Education in Jerusalem*, Evan S. Weiss

Volume Twenty-six
1   *Culture and Natural Environment: Ancient and Modern Middle Eastern Texts*, Sharif S. Elmusa, ed.
2   *Street Children in Egypt: Group Dynamics and Subcultural Constituents*, Nashaat Hussein
3   *IMF–Egyptian Debt Negotiations*, Bessma Momani
4   *Forced Migrants and Host Societies in Egypt and Sudan*, Fabienne Le Houérou

Volume Twenty-seven
1, 2   *Cultural Dynamics in Contemporary Egypt,* Maha Abdelrahman, Iman A. Hamdy, Malak Rouchdy, and Reem Saad (eds.)
3   *The Role of Local Councils in Empowerment and Poverty Reduction,* Solava Ibrahim
4   *Beach Politics: Gender and Sexuality in Dahab,* Mutafa Abdalla

Volume Twenty-eight
1   *Creating Families Across Boundaries: A Case Study of Romanian/Egyptian Mixed Marriages,* Ana Vinea
2, 3   *Pioneering Feminist Anthropology in Egypt: Selected Writings from Cynthia Nelson,* Martina Rieker, ed.
4   *Roses in Salty Soil: Women and Depression in Egypt Today.* Dalia A. Mostafa

Volume Twenty-nine
1   *Crossing Borders, Shifting Boundaries: Palestinian Dilemmas,* Sari Hanafi, ed.
2, 3   *Political and Social Protest in Egypt,* Nicholas S. Hopkins, ed.
4   *The Experience of Protest: Masculinity and Agency among Sudanese Refugees in Cairo,* Martin T. Rowe

Volume Thirty
1   *Child Protection Policies in Egypt: A Rights-Based Approach,* Adel Azer, Sohair Mehanna, Mulki Al-Sharmani, and Essam Ali
2   *"The Farthest Place": Social Boundaries in an Egyptian Desert Community,* Joseph Viscomi
3   *The New York Egyptians: Voyages and Dreams,* Yasmine M. Ahmed
4   *The Burden of Resources: Oil and Water in the Gulf and the Nile Basin,* Sharif S. Elmusa, ed.

Volume Thirty-one
1   *Humanist Perspectives on Sacred Space,* David Blanks, Bradley S. Clough, eds.
2   *Law as a Tool for Empowering Women within Marital Relations: A Case Study of Paternity Lawsuits in Egypt,* Hind Ahmed Zaki
3,4   *Visual Productions of Knowledge: Toward a Different Middle East,* Hanan Sabea, Mark R. Westmoreland, eds.

Volume Thirty-two
1   *Planning Egypt's New Settlements: The Politics of Spatial Inequities,* Dalia Wahdan

2   *Agrarian Transformation in the Arab World: Persistent and Emerging Challenges,* Habib Ayeb and Reem Saad
3   *Femininity and Dance in Egypt: Embodiment and Meaning in al-Raqs al-Baladi,* Noha Roushdy
4   *Negotiating Space: The Evolution of the Egyptian Street, 2000–2011,* Dimitris Soudias

Volume Thirty-three
1   *Masculinities in Egypt and the Arab World: Historical, Literary, and Social Science Perspectives,* Helen Rizzo, ed.
2   *Anthropology in Egypt 1900–1967: Culture, Function, and Reform,* Nicholas S. Hopkins
3   *The Church in the Square: Negotiations of Religion and Revolution at an Evangelical Church in Cairo,* Anna Jeannine Dowell
4   *The Political Economy of the New Egyptian Republic,* Nicholas S. Hopkins, ed.

Volume Thirty-four
1   *Egyptian Hip-Hop: Expressions From the Underground,* Ellen R. Weis

www.ingramcontent.com/pod-product-compliance
Lightning Source LLC
Chambersburg PA
CBHW070800040426
42333CB00060B/1724